THE PHILOSOPHERS

Borgo Press Books by CHARLES PALISSOT

The Philosophers & The Stumbling Block of Morals: Two Plays

THE PHILOSOPHERS

& THE STUMBLING BLOCK OF MORALS: TWO PLAYS

CHARLES PALISSOT

Translated and Adapted by Frank J. Morlock

THE BORGO PRESS
MMXIII

THE PHILOSOPHERS

Copyright © 2000, 2003, 2013 by Frank J. Morlock

FIRST EDITION

Published by Wildside Press LLC

www.wildsidebooks.com

DEDICATION

To Gerry Tetrault,
My Lifelong Friend and Philosopher

CONTENTS

THE PHILOSOPHERS. 9
CAST OF CHARACTERS. 10
ACT I 11
ACT II 34
ACT III 65
THE STUMBLING BLOCK OF MORALS . 103
CAST OF CHARACTERS. 104
ACT I 105
ACT II 127
ACT III 156
ABOUT THE TRANSLATOR. 176

THE PHILOSOPHERS

CAST OF CHARACTERS

CYDALISE

ROSALIE

DAMIS

VALÈRE

THEOPHRASTUS (Duclos)

DORTIDIUS (Diderot)

MARTON

CRISPIN

Mr. PROPICE, a Pedlar

Mr. CATONDAS

ACT I

The action takes place in Paris around 1760.

DAMIS:

No, I cannot get over such a shock. To break off a concluded marriage.

MARTON:

Everything is changed, I tell you.

DAMIS:

But still?

MARTON:

But still, you're an officer; our plan is not to involve ourselves in a mésalliance. We want a husband made of other stuff: and in a word, we will have a philosopher for a husband.

DAMIS:

What are you telling me, Marton?

MARTON:

I astonish you greatly? But don't you know that those who are absent are wrong? Three months have resulted in many changes. Perhaps in three months we shall see things otherwise, but until then—nothing. Despite the actions that ought to end in your marriage, today the apple is going to the philosopher. There's no appeal.

DAMIS:

They way they've changed so—in a moment.

MARTON:

Sir, every woman is a changeable creature. You could calculate Cydalise's age by the different tastes she's been seized with. Sometimes hair-brained, cheerful to excess, other times serious, and sulking in a fit. Coquettish she can be, even to the point of scandal. Prudish, to stun us with her strict morality; running to balls at night, sermons by day. Sometimes schoolmarms, sometimes clowns. Those were good times. But today, age gives way to other morals, and requires a wise tone. Madame has recently reformed her house a bit. We no longer rave wildly over the power of reason. First of all she's banished this vulgar frivolity, the delight of contractors, nourishment of the vulgar. At our proper suppers, the more we smile; if we are bored, at least it is with wit. Instead of vaudevilles, sometimes they allow concerts by savants, long, difficult tunes. For it still must be a bit amusing. But our strength, sir, is reasoning. Sometimes in the club we talk politics. In the end everything vanishes into metaphysics.

DAMIS:

This bizarre picture may be somewhat overburdened, but I remit Cydalise to strokes of your paint brush. What is Rosalie doing?

MARTON:

What we all do, sir. She's being bored.

DAMIS:

Has her sister surrendered herself to the vows of my rival?

MARTON:

No, her heart is yours. Love protected her against all the plans of a bold rival. But your fates depend on the conquest of her mother, who's bewitched to such a degree that I no longer hope. Pardon me that word. I see things the way I must see things.

DAMIS:

She was my friend and I flatter myself she still is.

MARTON:

Sir, all she adores is great wit. It's an illness unknown at twenty, but very common at fifty. Still, given time, one can hope for a return to wisdom. If there were someone to combat this weakness in the beginning before it progressed to such a degree, then I'd be hopeful. But, be aware of all our ills and those which will follow. Between you and me—

DAMIS:

Well, what?

MARTON:

Madame has written a book.

DAMIS:

Great!

MARTON:

Which she's printing up right now, incognito.

DAMIS:

Some pamphlet?

MARTON:

No, a full volume, in quarto.

DAMIS:

I will strongly advise her to keep it anonymous. But amongst these fine wits that Cydalise esteems is there no one, upright enough, frank enough, to show her the folly of such a great indiscretion? To disabuse her?

MARTON:

Them! They mock her. They all conspire to ruin her mind. Especially your rival: as he knows her taste, he doesn't limit himself to applauding everything. He makes her admired through his gentlemen yes-men. All clever charlatans, and agreeable flatterers. Delighted to preside in society, to bring their errors into it, and dominate a credulous mind by vanity that they skillfully insure against ridicule.

DAMIS:

And they are, you say, philosophers?

MARTON:

Yes, of the greatest airs. Paris is full of them. But, to better establish their credit with Madame, and to better penetrate to the depth of her soul, they name their choices to vacant jobs in the house, always guided by Healthy Reason, whatever that may be. It's always sure to please Madame. I still suspect a certain Secretary, received by Cydalise under the title scientist, of having never had any other employment than that of an intriguer, of concealing a cheat, and being here for some purpose. But anyway, sooner or later, I will clear the thing up.

DAMIS:

What motive do you have to judge so harshly?

MARTON:

Either I'm much mistaken, or it is your rival who, to serve his own turn, controls him.

DAMIS:

What kind of man is he?

MARTON:

A trickster, affecting frankness and yet, they tell me, a native of Pezinas, by the pompous name of Mr. Carondas, renowned as a scientist. At least he says so. All bristling with Greek and scholastic terms. Employing this bizarre jargon at every opportunity, and quoting Homer and Lycophon to us endlessly.

DAMIS:

(laughing) Ha, ha, ha, ha, ha, ha!

MARTON:

I'm painting according to Nature.

DAMIS:

This Mr. Carondas is a bad omen, but with your help and that of Crispin—

MARTON:

What? Crispin is here?

DAMIS:

Yes, truly. My plan was to unite you, you know that. And I hope you will give me your best service.

MARTON:

Leave me alone for that. Crispin is very clever. I'll turn that cleverness to good account.

DAMIS:

I am counting on your efforts.

MARTON:

Oh, sir, you may. I am declaring war on philosophy.

DAMIS:

I owe you my life's happiness, Marton. But can't I get a moment—?

MARTON:

Ah! I saw you coming. Hold on, sir. Love knows how to foresee you. She's coming. It's Rosalie.

(Rosalie enters)

DAMIS:

After three months' absence, when I return here I hope to reclaim an oath that was promised to my ardor. Now, I'm told that a rival envious of my happiness dares contest with me the only treasure I desire, and that your mother dares conspire with him against me. Ah, at least reassure my despairing heart.

ROSALIE:

Do you doubt that mine is less penetrated? Sadly, I see

this extreme change: I am suffering as much as you. But still, I love you, under which title at least some hope is allowed me. Who can resist two joined lovers? My mother loves you. Perhaps seeing your friendship toward me will rekindle love in her embattled heart, just as previously I had more power over it; it's you, Damis, who must move her. Go, and I will owe it to my mother to complete this happiness I hope for.

MARTON:

Nice sentiments, but as for me, I am not relying on them.

ROSLIE:

Leave me in my error.

MARTON:

No, it's by means of confrontations we must bring Cydalise back to reason.

DAMIS:

Still, attempting the enterprise is permitted.

MARTON:

Yes, sighs and tears are a fine way. Oh, philosophy really hardens hearts.

ROSALIE:

I wouldn't have believed it! But still, if my mother immolates me without return to the designs of Valère, if, finally, this plan was really tested, why, up to now, hasn't it been declared? What's holding it back?

MARTON:

I'm getting furious! It's true that as yet she hasn't sent for the notary, the witnesses have not been invited. It still lacks formalities, I agree. Add further that the day has not been strictly determined, Again, I agree. All the same, doesn't she suffer a sufficiently public homage that he pays to your attractions? Aren't you beset right now? No, indeed, I'm mistaken, it's just a passing thought.

ROSALIE:

Alas, Marton, how can you desolate me like this?

MARTON:

I was dreaming.

DAMIS:

Marton—!

MARTON:

Stories here and there, things in the air!

DAMIS:

Marton—

MARTON:

Hallucinations, absurdities!

ROSALIE:

But, Marton—

MARTON:

No, it's panic, illusions, I tell you.

ROSALIE:

Really, Marton. This cruel jesting is not really in season.

MARTON:

I was wrong.

ROSALIE:

(starting to leave) You're going to keep it up? Well, I—

DAMIS:

(stopping her) Rosalie—

ROSALIE:

No, sir, it's too much.

DAMIS:

Stay, I beg you.

MARTON:

Ah! So, you are getting annoyed? Really, that's very well done. Why, let's reason a bit. Tell me, if you please, do I have to deceive you? I know quite well that skepticism suspends the impressions of evils that one questions. It's very natural to separate the danger. And to always make your burden lighter, I would be the first to flatter you, to shut your eyes to the light. But the urgent interest that makes me speak for you— Pardon, but my word, lovers are mad. Complaisant for no reason, desperate without cause, in a state of equilibrium that knows no rest, while a cool head often advises better than love, which paints a blindfold over their eyes.

DAMIS:

What! Now, there's philosophy!

MARTON:

In the country they say you learn to howl with the wolves! The proverb is correct. It's an evil spread throughout the house. Let's put aside this troublesome idea (to Rosalie) for the moment. There! Let's make peace. You won't be rancorous, you promise me?

ROSALIE:

Ah, I promise you.

MARTON:

And I to be attentive to all your interests. You, sir, who would like to spend your life staring at Miss, must beat a retreat, and very promptly. Consider, it's broad daylight, and that we risk being surprised here, and that, first of all, you must present yourself to Cydalise before thinking of any other meeting.

DAMIS:

I am rushing to present myself in so sweet a hope. I am placing my happiness in life in your hands. You, who I adore, my dear Rosalie—goodbye!

(exit Damis)

MARTON:

As for you, don't be weak. Come on, no moping. To

misfortune oppose determination.

ROSALIE:

If you could just feel how much I hate Valère!

MARTON:

Yes, Damis is gone. It's to your mother that you must speak with fire. When you loved Damis, I suppose she approved it.

ROSALIE:

Certainly.

MARTON:

Everyone knows girls do nothing without family advice. That's the rule. You have to declare without any evasion: your love for one and your scorn for the other.

ROSALIE:

Oh, yes.

MARTON:

You feel this firmness of mind in you?

ROSALIE:

Assuredly, Marton.

MARTON:

(maliciously) Get ready. I hear Madame.

ROSALIE:

(terrified) Ah, Marton!

MARTON:

What? This is a fine beginning! It promises well.

ROSALIE:

So why scare me? Love will supply me with courage when I need it!

MARTON:

Love! Yes, you will both make a mess of things. Or so it appears, really, from this air of fright over a word said by chance.

ROSALIE:

But in the end you will see.

MARTON:

Love won't get you out of trouble; love is very clumsy. Think of your hate. That's the feeling that ought to inspire you—you must really be filled with it, that's important. Much as I revere it, I don't know if love is the most costly of our passions, but it is the weakest, and it makes you timid. Hate is all ardor and excitement. Love dispirits, hate animates. And in a female heart, my word, I would think it much more natural. May your heart prove itself today. See, I love Crispin, and for Valère I feel—but this is too much. I see your mother.

ROSALIE:

You will support me?

MARTON:

Yes.

CYDALISE: (entering)

Withdraw, Marton. Go lock up my Plato with his world of ideas. My head is numb. I am expecting my Encyclopedia any moment. That book must not leave my office. (to Rosalie) You, stay. I want to speak to you in secret. (to Marton) Leave us.

MARTON: (to Rosalie)

Come on, be firm and show some courage.

CYDALISE:

Obey, Marton.

(exit Marton.)

You are beautiful and wise, Rosalie, and I've always been generous to you. At last I am going to know if you deserve it. I am not consulting that vulgar sentiment: love of choice—trivial, popular, which they say stems from the blood speaking in us, and which at bottom is only a lie, however sweet, and a weakness.

ROSALIE:

Eh! What, the voice of nature. This pure and touching impression. This first of duties, this splendid chain. I am only describing what I feel keenly. No matter! Can it be that today my mother's heart denies this sacred character? Ah, remember your past feelings and by analyzing them, you will weaken.

CYDALISE:

Like everybody else, I believe in those vain chimeras that ruled our fathers as worthy ideas of great good sense. Credulous, happy even in my blindness, an abused automaton, I followed the flood. I began to feel, to think, to know. If, in the end, I love you, it's in quality of Being. But, you conceive clearly, that another individual would have less extensive right to my bounty.

ROSALIE:

You are tearing my heart apart! Ah, madame, allow me—suffer that your daughter reclaim at your knees a more legitimate right and gentler titles. Why break the ties that attach me to you? Judge their power by my trouble and my tears.

CYDALISE: (a bit moved)

My daughter! What! Your error has so many charms! You make me pity you. Consult reason. Their puerilities are not in season. I recognize your claims on a mother's heart. But I demystify them, and if I am dear to you, if in my turn, I also have some rights, I exclude chance which gave you birth.

ROSALIE:

I cannot keep up this funereal language; it outrages both of us. Who? Me? Do you think I can ever forget that my life is one of your bounties? No—

CYDALISE:

You should be especially grateful for the care I've taken with your intelligence. That's the worthy object towards which all my desires bend. What I wish is to teach you to think. Imagine the happiness of hearing his genius, of opening your eyes to the clarity of philosophy, of dissipating the night into which your feelings are plunged. Of freeing your mind from the yoke of prejudice. This great ace of existence which belongs only to a savant, whose firm advantage I know at last, this day of reason which I've been enlightened by. Daughter, my love wants to prove it for you. I have concluded your marriage with Damis. Trivial interests determined me to end a lawsuit, the similarities of fortune. I remembered that everything seemed to unite you. That's the way most business is concluded. But today I am smashing these vulgar chains. Damis has good sense, virtues, honor. He has what the world demands in minute detail. But all mortals are not meant to reach the sublime. At bottom, still, one must esteem him. But, I owe you another spouse, my daughter! One much more worthy of you, and more fitting. Valère has what it takes to please and seduce. He will know how to lead you from that point to the little more required to love. And in a word, my heart has chosen him.

ROSALIE:

Thus you are forgetting that in the past Damis had your consent and that of my father?

CYDALISE:

Your father! It's true, I wasn't thinking of him. A

pleasant authority indeed! The most narrow-minded being Nature ever made. No talent, no flair, a kind of machine functioning by habit and thinking by routine. Seeming to dream, yet thinking of nothing. Gravely occupied with the details of his profession, and a thousand other purely domestic cares. Boring, defender of Gothic prejudices, savage in his manners. The cut of his clothes, the most bourgeois fashion. Ever declaiming with gravity and severity, and who always leaned on the magistracy outside his court room. One would think him stooped over, having a jury to judge.— But he's dead now, let's leave him in peace.

ROSALIE:

Ah, Madame, I think—

CYDALISE:

Are you going to defend him? A father is only a man, and one can reasonably speak about his faults—when speaking openly.

ROSALIE:

If these are the rights of philosophy, suffer me to renounce them, and for all my life. I would lose too much, Madame, by being enlightened like this. I dare confess it to you. Also, deign to permit me to again remind you your first kindness implored your daughter in favor of Damis.

CYDALISE:

No. Valère is the lover I have chosen for you, and as of tonight, he will be your spouse. This connection will embellish the course of your life. As to your prejudices against philosophy, you must be hardened against them by my example. Time and reason will cure you of it. You are of that age when one begins to live. Everything's unclear to you, but you will read my book. In it, I treat briefly wit, good sense, the passions, law. government, virtue, morality, climate, customs, civilized nations and savages, apparent disorder and universal order, ideal good and virtual good. Carefully, I examine the principles of things. The linkage of causes and secret effects. Expressly for you I wrote a profound chapter I intend to title: Duties, Such as They Are. Finally, it's a moral encyclopedia. Valère describes it as a book of genius. You will be very happy with such a spouse. One day you will understand what I am doing for you and you will than, me. Goodbye, Miss: think of obeying me.

(Cydalise leaves.)

ROSALIE: (without seeing Marton)

What mortal sadness! What to decide? What to do? Ah, there you are, Marton.

MARTON:

Yes, I heard everything. But what foolishness, what rashness!

ROSALIE:

There's nothing left for me but to die.

MARTON:

Banter! Die! You're joking and that's no longer customary. They don't allow it even in Romance novels!

ROSALIE:

But, still—

MARTON:

Calm down and get your sense back. After all, you were expecting this crisis.

ROSALIE:

At the moment, my soul is no less moved.

MARTON:

Do you expect so little of my efforts?

ROSALIE:

Ah, Marton!

MARTON:

Begin by afflicting yourself less. Tell me: if your wishes are fulfilled, what use will all this fine gloom be?

ROSALIE:

Ah, if you succeed. But who will guarantee me that?

MARTON:

Then you can cry as much as you like! I will even help you, and will have nothing to say. But until then, who forbids you to laugh? In any event, it's still very well done. And if all goes ill, I think it's necessary. That's my humor. Besides, gloom bothers me: I think it's useless. And I am the opposite pole from it. In life one must never think that way. And it's always wrong to afflict oneself. But let's go cook up some happy sally. Come, and we will see if philosophy, whatever its credit, can, in broad daylight, hold out against me, Marton, Crispin, and Love.

CURTAIN

ACT II

VALÈRE:

Frontin!

CARONDAS:

That cursed name will cause some great mistake. I've said so, and in front of Cydalise. It will happen to you for calling me thus. Frontin! Fine name for a savant. Think of it. Sir, it was only necessary for this stupidity to bring down philosophy.

VALÈRE:

Right you are.

CARONDAS:

Anyway, between ourselves even, we must suppress these too demeaning tones, since, according to you, men are equal by Natural Law. Therefore I am, although Frontin, your equal!

VALÈRE:

I swear to you that is my feeling.

CARONDAS:

As for me, I approve it strongly. I've always thought that the laws were wrong, and even Cydalise in a certain chapter, doesn't prove it too badly—to my taste.

VALÈRE:

The vain title, the opinion of a mad woman who in a moment would adopt a completely different opinion. She knows only words and has nothing in her head.

CARONDAS:

But, between ourselves, sir, is her book really so stupid?

VALÈRE:

Pitiful!

CARONDAS:

The style?

VALÈRE:

Excessively boring.

CARONDAS:

Still, you flatter her with the most brilliant success.

VALÈRE:

Doubtless.

CARONDAS:

And the public?

VALÈRE:

We know how to direct it as to how it must think, speak, judge, write. We will easily control it.

CARONDAS:

Right, but you have to appease it, flatter it.

VALÈRE:

No, never. There are more certain methods of winning it.

CARONDAS:

The means?

VALÈRE:

For example—insulting it. It's an expedient that our

sages devised: the secret is sure, we've tested it. In short, you will witness it with surprise: we will carry Cydalise's name to heaven. Five or six elements—bold, revolting, scandalous—will produce a marvelous effect in her book. We have to add them.

CARONDAS:

Fine! It's a novel trick. And how to prove these elements are from her?

VALRERE:

First of all, she'll defend herself out of modesty. Then she'll think she's the author.

CARONDAS:

I don't know. But as for me, my soul would blush.

VALÈRE:

Have you forgotten that Cydalise is a woman? Believe me, imagine even the crudest trap, vanity is credulous and you can trust in it; on this point, women are sincere enough.

CARONDAS:

Clever, witty gentlemen owe nothing to them. But still, you think by adding five or six passages we must attain the most happy success?

VALÈRE:

Doubtless, and between ourselves, this idea is not new. Crates' book—wasn't that the proof? No production ever soared so high. It was all the rage, and it's still all the rage. Because everywhere it's treated as a dangerous book. And yet we know Crates is a good man.

CARONDAS:

It's true.

VALÈRE:

Cydalise will have great favor. Her sex is never judged harshly. Some of the features whispered in the ear will make the besotted public cry, "Marvel!" My intention is for even Crates to be jealous. And nothing is easier. We will all protect her.

CARONDAS:

Well, sir, although nourished in your school, I had, on my honor, quite honest admiration for the work of the author. But still, word for word, she's written nothing, only copied you.

VALÈRE:

The idiot.

CARONDAS:

But as to the beautiful items added to her book: what if the laws decide to pursue us, sir?

VALÈRE:

She will have the pleasure of hearing herself praised, right? Worry about disavowing it all later. Besides, love of truth is pursued to the point of heroism. Those grand imposing words of error—to fanaticism. Persecution comes to her aid. It's a resource which always succeeds. Don't we have the example of Socrates, oppressed, condemned by his ungrateful country? All our admirers will be speaking at once.

CARONDAS:

But, sir, Socrates obeyed the laws.

VALÈRE:

Yes, philosophy, still in its infancy, kept up appearances at least. But we don't want to do that anymore.

CARONDAS:

Then everything has become permissible.

VALÈRE:

Except against us and against our friends.

CARONDAS:

Long live fine wit and philosophy! There is no better invention to sweeten life.

VALÈRE:

(enthusiastically) What! You place Virtue on the Rocks. Let whoever can climb, go up there. Man was ignorant, this king of beasts, without guide, without compass. Wandering on the ocean of the world at the whim of the wind. But now we know what his true propeller is: man is always led on by the attraction of happiness; it is in his passions that it finds its source. Without them, the body stops in its course, languishing sadly, attached to the earth. This unknown power, this hidden principle, only Philosophy was able to reveal. And morality itself must submit to genius. On the globe on which we live, the universal despot is merely a single means: personal interest. Over all our feelings that alone presides. That alone lights us in our choice and guides us free of prejudices. But tractable to its voice, the attentive savage follows it in the depths of his forests. Civilized men recognize its empire. In a word, it rules all who breathe,

CARONDOS:

What, sir! Interest alone must be heard?

VALÈRE:

Nature has made it a necessity.

CARONDAS:

I have some regret about deceiving Cydalise, but clearly see the thing is permitted.

VALÈRE:

Fortune calls you, you must take it at its word.

CARONDAS:

Yes, sir.

VALÈRE:

Frankness is the virtue of a fool.

CARONDAS: (putting himself in a position to steal from Valère)

Yes, sir. But still I feel some scruple which would stop me.

VALÈRE:

Ridiculous prejudice which must be gotten rid of.

CARONDAS:

What, truly?

VALÈRE:

It's a question of being happy, no matter how.

CARONDAS:

In earnest?

VALÈRE:

Why, without a doubt. By flattering Cydalise you fulfill a duty authorized by custom. Don't you have to flatter when you want to please people? Really, to see one's interests is to have good sense. The superfluity of fools is our patrimony. What the pirate said to Alexander the Great, is, at bottom, true.

CARONDAS: (picking Valère's pocket)

Yes, sir.

VALÈRE:

All wealth ought to become common—why, it is the means of avenging oneself on fate. With shrewdness and dexterity one can correct one's star, and it's a weakness to be tormented by a scruple. (noticing Carandos is picking his pocket) Why, what are you up to there?

CARONDAS:

Personal interest, that hidden principal, sir, which inspires us, and which rules all that breathes.

VALÈRE:

What, traitor, steal from me?

CARONDAS:

No, I am exercising my right. All wealth is common.

VALÈRE:

Yes, but be more dexterous. There are certain unpleasantries to which one is exposed when one is caught.

CARONDAS:

Sir, I'll be careful of that.

VALÈRE:

This, Mr. Frontin, must be a lesson. But since we must no longer call you by this name, think of helping me with Cydalise. Up to this point all is going well. Her daughter is promised to me. You know what my feelings are on that subject. So continue to flatter her talents. Your term "colleague" has produced marvels. We must increasingly deafen her ears with this scientific jargon which you employ. You being without fortune can still create a small position which I will take pains to prolong if my prayers have the effect I have the right to expect. Goodbye, be discreet, I will be generous.

(exit Valère)

CARONDAS: (alone)

My first attempt wasn't so lucky. I am still far from equaling my model. And it is to the second rank that destiny calls me.

CYDALISE: (entering without seeing Carondas)

Here I am come to rid myself of the heaviest imaginable idleness. In the midst of all those bores, I was obsessed. I didn't glimpse the germ of an idea. They outrage good sense to such a degree; but one has to put with these relatives. (to Carondas) Ah, you are here! Good, take your seat. My book is going to appear. They are waiting for the preface. I've got to work on it. I wish we had Valère here.

CARONDAS:

He just now left me. And we were speaking of you, Madame, with intoxication.

CYDALISE:

You were speaking of my book?

CARONDAS:

He spoke of it ceaselessly. It is, he says, a certificate of immortality. You are going to eclipse the learned of ancient times. I don't dare compare my enthusiasm with his, but I am taken with admiration at every page.

CYDALISE:

You are satisfied with it?

CARONDAS:

My soul is confounded by it. Your book is nourished in such a deep understanding that you will make me believe in the Demon of Socrates.

CYDALISE:

You understand it?

CARONDAS:

Yes, Madame, I flatter myself I do. But tell me how it was done. You must know everything to write as you've written.

CYDALISE:

With the number of people I've met, and pure chance.

CARONDAS:

You were inspired. What, you haven't read the savant Vossuis?

CYDALISE:

No, never.

CARONDAS:

Casaubon?

CYDALISE:

Even less.

CARONDAS:

Grotius?

CYDALISE:

Not at all. Are those books for a woman?

CARONDAS:

My word, you astonish me more and more. Madame, what? None of all that?

CYDALISE:

Why, you talk of laws better than Tribonian. Oh, at

CARONDAS:

He spoke of it ceaselessly. It is, he says, a certificate of immortality. You are going to eclipse the learned of ancient times. I don't dare compare my enthusiasm with his, but I am taken with admiration at every page.

CYDALISE:

You are satisfied with it?

CARONDAS:

My soul is confounded by it. Your book is nourished in such a deep understanding that you will make me believe in the Demon of Socrates.

CYDALISE:

You understand it?

CARONDAS:

Yes, Madame, I flatter myself I do. But tell me how it was done. You must know everything to write as you've written.

CYDALISE:

With the number of people I've met, and pure chance.

CARONDAS:

You were inspired. What, you haven't read the savant Vossuis?

CYDALISE:

No, never.

CARONDAS:

Casaubon?

CYDALISE:

Even less.

CARONDAS:

Grotius?

CYDALISE:

Not at all. Are those books for a woman?

CARONDAS:

My word, you astonish me more and more. Madame, what? None of all that?

CYDALISE:

Why, you talk of laws better than Tribonian. Oh, at

least admit Tribonian—

CYDALISE:

I am unaware of him.

CARONDAS:

At least you're familiar with Thales, Anaxagoras?

CYDALISE:

No.

CARONDAS:

"The Natural Son?"

CYDALISE:

As to that, yes. They are writings which must be cited first of all.

CARONDAS:

I don't wish to set myself up as an arbiter, but I would have judged the title as you.

CYDALISE:

That's also my opinion. And I think that an excellent work announces itself in its least feature. It's an…I don't know what. Our soul is ravished by it, it feels it, it's the attraction of genius.

CARONDAS:

I understand. It's almost like the vapor of a stew which at the same time appeals to your sense of smell and taste.

CYDALISE:

Yes, although the comparison is rather vulgar.

CARONDAS:

It's from Lycophon.

CYDALISE:

Ah, that's another matter. Let me get back to my preface. Come on, I am going to dictate. (after a silence and with some emphasis) Write: "I've lived." No, that's a bad opening. Erase: "I've lived." Relax (sharply) Ah, Mr. Carondas, your pen is bad. (she ponders) "I've lived" is no good.

CARONDAS:

To the contrary, I think "I've lived" says a lot.

CYDALISE:

No, sir. I want an opening that's more pompous and philosophic.

CARONDAS:

Madame, simplicity is energetic.

CYDALISE: (pondering)

No, no, I'm searching for a phrase that may be less familiar. (bitterly) I've never written on such paper. Erase it, sir. Your ink is detestable. (pondering) Shall I never find a more favorable phrase? (impatiently) Ah, after all Valère really ought to be here. I never feel so much wit as when I am with him. (pondering) What? Not even one idea? Ah, I'm being tortured.

CARONDAS:

Madame, genius has its caprices. And this reminds me of a saying by Suidas, who says elegantly—

CYDALISE:

Eh, Mr. Carondas, leave the dead in peace. I just had a sublime phrase which escapes me. (dreamily) Wait, why yes, this phrase expresses— (impatiently) Write! No! The phrase is very obscure. I've never felt so sterile. What a job. Let's be done with it. I renounce it. The printer is waiting. Take him my reply. No! Come back. Finally, I've found it. I've got it. Quickly, sir, Write: "Young man, take this and read!" The phrase is unique. What do you think of it, sir?

CARONDAS:

Sublime, magnificent! It has the tone of genius and truth.

CYDALISE:

I was forgetting, reading it, all that it has cost me. "Young man, take this and read!" It's inimitable. And Valère will be incredibly overjoyed with it.

CARONDAS:

By a sweet tingling that you feel troubling you— "Young man, take this and read"—the oracle is going to speak. Nature is manifesting itself here, before your eyes. No, Nothing is so sublime, and yet so modest.

CYDALISE:

But what does Marton want with us?

MARTON:

(entering) Madame, it's Damis who is asking to see you.

CYDALISE:

What a bad time for him to come! I was going to finish without him. This importunate character won't allow me to complete a work.

MARTON:

Valère will finish it.

CARONDAS:

What do you mean finish? The work is complete, Madame, and can never be equaled. Our greatest geniuses cannot do as much in ten years.

CYDALISE:

Yes, you're right. Make twenty copies. Ah, finally, I can breathe again. And I knew how to manage it: "Young man, take this and read!" Yes, Damis can come in.

(exit Carondas and Marton. Then Damis enters.)

CYDALISE:

So you've returned?

DAMIS:

Yes, I'm back and I'm opening my soul to you. I perceive only too well, and with sorrow, that I've lost my rights in the depth of your heart. You know to what degree your daughter is dear to me. It's your vow, or at least that of her father, that I reclaim today in favor of my passion. Sure now, I need some support.

CYDALISE:

I confess the title is legitimate enough. I admit my wrongdoing. Not that my esteem or my friendship that attaches me to you, or even my feelings which remain so tender: and that's what I ought to say to you first of all. But I've formed connections whose charm attracts me. Too long I've pursued frivolous errors of a world I loved. Age has changed my mores. Today I am made completely for philosophy. Free of prejudices that corrupted my life, and now I exist only for the truth. A not very populous company, it's true. I live with sages and am learning to think from reading their works. From amongst them, I've chosen one for my daughter. And this evening, this happy evening, must fulfill my dream. It's for me to judge, if, although your friend, I must sacrifice you to my life's happiness.

DAMIS:

No, I'd give my life for your happiness. And your friendship always inspires me. But what are these truly rare advantages you speak of, attached to intercourse with sages? I don't hold for such a bunch of charlatans that one sees amusing passersby on the stage, who place a blemish on their philosophy. My reason deifies all these self-important characters whose vainglorious appearance seduces the vulgar. I am one of those people who set little store by reputation, and I distinguish carefully between the friend of wisdom and the pedant who grows hoarse endlessly preaching.

CYDALISE:

I know all the scorn that pedants deserve. I don't confuse them with real savants. Spare yourself this bitter satire, sir. Those that I can name—Theophrastus, Valère, Dortidius—are all quite well known.

DAMIS:

I didn't know that Dortidius was one of them. What, Madame, he's involved?

CYDALISE:

Why so surprised?

DAMIS:

I know him, I tell you. Excuse my frankness, apparently he hides his schemes well. But he's only a fool, almost by his own admission. Someone made me see him, and, despite his grimace and the empty compliments he pays you, and the sugary affection of his honeyed proposals— My word, I saw nothing very miraculous, despite his capable tone and his hypocritical air, I was not tempted to believe in his worth and to depict him briefly, I find in him only a cold enthusiasm that imposes only on fools.

CYDALISE:

That judgment wrongs your intelligence, and Dortidius does honor to France. His name among the savants is always in credit, and I don't know why everybody speaks ill of him. But let's leave this matter. These rare advantages which I owe to trafficking with sages I ought to tell you about, and do them honor for it. Perhaps after that you will be fair to them. Never mind! You must at least learn to know them. I held prejudices which degraded my being. Vainly my reason wanted to emancipate itself. Habit soon plunged me into them again. The silliest terrors declared war on me. I believed in ghosts, I was afraid of thunder. I blush before these absurdities. But they cradled us in this nonsense, and the impression is only more durable. Our frivolous, despicable education, far from enlightening us to the truth, has only the dangerous effect of masking our mistakes. I owe a new being to these divine men. Chance presided over my attachments, I was full of attention for my relatives, and the degrees between them regulated my preferences. This order extended even to our acquaintances. I had all these bad habits and many others still. Finally, my feelings took another flight. My wit, purified by philosophy, sees the universe in large, and adopts it for its country Putting my sensibility to profit, I no longer am tender for anything but humanity.

DAMIS:

Madame, I don't know, but even if I must displease you, this word "Humanity" no longer imposes on me. And hearing it repeated by so many cheats, I think that they are conspiring to have it adopted. They have some interest to put it in fashion. It's a veil, at once honorable and convenient, masking the nullity of their feelings, lending a beautiful exterior to their emptiness. I've little seen these folks who ceaselessly extol tenderness show more tenderness for unfortunates, show themselves, at need, more fervent friends by being more generous or more compassionate, giving less importance to attacking good deeds, or showing more indulgence to the faults of others, and consoling merit and seeking the means to become, in a word, better citizens. And to speak the truth, I suspect them of loving "mankind," but actually loving no one.

CYDALISE:

You've really got it in for this humanity.

DAMIS:

It's too much abused, and I am revolted. It's too vast a feeling for the heart of man. Sometimes, by way of pleasant contrast, I've seen the very warmest partisans of this extreme system cherish the whole universe: except their children!

CYDALISE:

Truly, sir, the sages have something to complain about: you are an adversary to be feared by them. It's vain for the century and the nation to applaud them for the good they've done. They would have done better to remain deaf and serve as the interpreters and organ of envy.

DAMIS:

And what good has this philosophy produced? I don't discover its shining successes. I see around me small, self-important creatures, who, to have a style, enroll in a sect, thinking thereby to lose their character as insects, believing themselves to be a court, and become admirers and protectors of art: to art's ruin! Not alive to satire, and detecting nothing in these outbursts of laughter, in all places they still see themselves pursued; preferring to the honor of serving their country, the condition of colporteurs of philosophy. Are these the successes in which they glorify themselves?

CYDALISE:

I admire your reasons, they are of great weight. And you cite me some choice examples indeed worthy of supporting your cause. But does abuse ever prove anything? Must it be renounced because of bores?

DAMIS:

Madame, these abuses are becoming very common. I foresee strange disasters for morality, and I am alarmed by many philosophers.

CYDALISE:

Remain, sir, remain in your opinion. It's not to be remedied by prevention. You would have a scruple to think otherwise. Eh! What can reason do about a credulous mind?

DAMIS:

You think you've said it all with that word, Madame. Credulity has become the equivalent of folly. Indeed, to the eyes of many folk, at least, the matter is clear. These people will never persuade me. And their jesting tone will never frighten me. I have my opinion, and if I displease, I lament it. But over them I think what must be thought. I dare to declare it, I must do it, and I glory in it. These gentlemen can laugh, but without humiliating me. They have been given the right to make themselves gay. But for me, I dare in my turn to find them ridiculous, and often stupidity makes men incredulous.

CYDALISE:

That's speaking wisely! I applaud you for it. It's well

done of you, just to have an opinion. But without getting lost in these lofty matters, I know what I owe to talent, to luminaries, to those men that you persecute.

DAMIS:

They've taught you great things? I don't believe it. They have the art of destruction, but they don't grow anything, and not to instruct. What fruit do you expect from their vain arguments? I see only too many afflicting effects. You will follow in their steps from sophism to sophism. You will be lost in the night of sorrowing skepticism.[1] Ah, Madame, renounce these agitators. They are the one who ought to be called persecutors. Abjure an error which is foreign to you, and return at last to your true character.

CYDALISE:

Have you said everything? I admire the good sense and solidity of your reasoning. Your desert shines with a very high polish. But I've made my decision. You'll never have my daughter. Goodbye, sir.

(Cydalise leaves)

DAMIS:

Ah, heaven! I don't know where I am.

(Enter Crispin)

---

1. Pyrrhonism in original.

CRISPIN:

Well, has this proceeding born happy fruits? Are we getting married, sir? Cydalise doubtless—

DAMIS:

I've just spoken to her, Crispin. But what it cost me. I have to renounce this marriage.

CRISPIN:

What's this?

DAMIS:

I am dismissed.

CRISPIN:

What? Indeed! Formally?

DAMIS:

Yes, Crispin, quite formally.

CRISPIN:

Sir, we know how to please. And we've been shown the door by Valère. Is there no remedy?

DAMIS:

I don't see any.

CRISPIN:

Right! You cannot think of one. As for me, I see a hundred instead of one. Quite simply we must carry off Rosalie. That's the easiest thing to do.

DAMIS:

What an excess of madness! Do you think she would consent to it? You know her better than to talk to me like this.

CRISPIN:

I like this way, but since it displeases you we shall have recourse to surer means. I will go find Valère, and I will speak to him in a way that makes him desert this house tonight.

DAMIS:

That would indeed be the wisest way—but Cydalise—

CRISPIN:

Well?

DAMIS:

—Cydalise will see only an outrage in it, and that is precisely the way to exasperate her. The secret of ruining me without hope of recovery.

CRISPIN:

All right—then I with lucid audacity will enlighten Cydalise, and chase out all these prattlers who ruin wit. I have some credit with her in my turn, and, with Marton seconding the enterprise a little, you'll soon see her submit to reason.

DAMIS: (overjoyed at first)

Ah, Crispin. (dejected) But how can I rely on you?

CRISPIN:

I want her to choose between Valère and me. You don't know all my merits yet. You are looking at a new Aristotle.

DAMIS:

You?

CRISPIN:

Myself, sir. I've done more than one profession. A wise man deigned to associate me in his work, and someday my name would have been on the list—at least he flattered me by saying so when I was his copyist.

DAMIS:

What?

CRISPIN:

I actually had several admirers. Ah, what a wrong he did me by avoiding honors to live in the woods. I must do him the justice that he never used trickery or artifice in his philosophy. At bottom, he was bull-headed, full of rectitude and sincerity, a beast at once misanthropic and cynical. He was really a madman, unique in his species.

DAMIS:

Ah, can I listen to you in the trouble I am in?

MARTON: (entering)

Come, sir. You must lighten up these troubles. Quick, some gaiety.

DAMIS:

Why? What do you mean?

MARTON:

First of all, sir, I mean to begin laughing at them.

CRISPIN:

Yes, let's laugh. That's well said.

DAMIS:

I am in despair!

MARTON:

Good! You mustn't think about it and don't look too darkly.

CRISPIN:

Why, indeed, I think she's got some vertigo.

MARTON:

Console yourself.

DAMIS:

Marton.

MARTON:

Console yourself, I tell you.

DAMIS:

What's happened?

MARTON:

You are going to learn. Come. Yes, I am going to put you in the ranks of fortunate lovers.

CURTAIN

ACT III

DAMIS:

I cannot yet get over my surprise. So this is how they're deceiving Cydalise.

MARTON:

I hope that in the end she'll listen to reason.

DAMIS:

Oh! No longer doubt it, this letter is very good! What won't I give you for this happy discovery?

MARTON:

Great luck, sir, that this door is opening! My word, I was on the lookout for it, and for a long while I always said he was one of that sort. I would have sworn it.

CRISPIN:

It names Frontin. I recognized the man from the name alone.

MARTON:

But who will undertake to present this document?

DAMIS:

You?

MARTON:

Me? Sir, I'd be ruining myself in her opinion. I would never dare.

DAMIS:

Marton.

MARTON:

A letter in this style, to my mistress! Oh, no! No weakness! It would cost me too much.

DAMIS:

But—

MARTON:

Unnecessary talk. I won't do it.

DAMIS:

Nor I—

CRISPIN:

Me, neither.

MARTON:

Besides, it has to be returned in their presence or we have nothing.

DAMIS:

Certainly.

CRISPIN:

Silence. Cydalise, I believe, has never seen me.

MARTON:

No.

CRISPIN:

And I am unknown throughout the house?

MARTON:

Yes.

CRISPIN:

I intend to introduce myself and please her. Give me that letter. I'll take this business on myself. Go, sir. I'll know how to serve you.

MARTON:

But really, I predict that it can succeed.

CRISPIN:

I want Marton for the price of my services. What wouldn't I dare under like omens?

MARTON:

They're coming. It's the assembly. You two be off!

DAMIS:

I confide the success of my hopes to your efforts.

MARTON:

Eh! Quick, be off for fear off surprise.

(exit Damis and Crispin. After a moment the philosophers enter. Marton makes a deep curtsy)

MARTON:

Gentlemen, I am going to announce you to Cydalise.

(exit Marton)

THEOPHRASTUS: (to Valère)

Well? The marriage is finally decided?

VALÈRE:

Yes, I'm marrying tonight. The Notary's been sent for.

DORTIDIUS:

By Jove, I am ravished.

THEOPHRASTUS:

How I congratulate you.

DORTIDIUS:

My word. This fortune is owed to your merit.

THEOPHRASTUS:

Yes, despite the scorn of all the envious.

DORTIDIUS:

At bottom, you could hope for much better.

VALÈRE:

Gentlemen.

DORTIDIUS:

No, I mean it, and no flattery.

VALÈRE:

You wish—

DORTIDIUS:

We know how to honor your genius.

VALÈRE:

Ah, you are confusing me with all these compliments.

DORTIDIUS:

Why, it's the truth.

VALÈRE:

If I had your talents, if I were renowned with your sublime qualities, this praise would become legitimate.

THEOPHRASTUS:

And the intended consents at last?

VALÈRE:

With regret. But what causes me to secretly displease her?

THEOPHRASTUS:

Doubtless with time you will render her docile.

DORTIDIUS:

It must be that Rosalie is difficult to please.

VALÈRE:

I don't know what rival disputes for her heart with me. But, in the end, Cydalise is only more ardent.

DORTIDIUS:

(laughing) Cydalise, you agree the dupe is really good.

VALÈRE:

As soon as the marriage is over, I will abandon her to you. I'd die if the affair were prolonged a long while. Never have people been bored to this degree.

DORTIDIUS:

As for me, on honor, once your marriage is concluded, I will withdraw.

THEOPHRASTUS:

My word, I'm leaving, too. The means suffice. (to Valère) You, at least, vain, animated by hope, give yourself a reason to be bored by duty and love.

VALÈRE: (laughing)

Yes, love. That's really what tempts me.

DORTIDIUS:

By God, he's marrying one thousand shillings of income.

VALÈRE: (to Theophrastus)

What then! Do you find me of an amorous cast? That would be ridiculously frightful at my age. These days people are returning to that vulgar error, and they think of pleasure, but only after fortune.

THEOPHRASTUS:

He's right.

DORTIDIUS:

I think like him.

VALÈRE:

Without it, how else could I support the boredom that endlessly obsessed me around that mad woman? Oh, I wouldn't take to such bad habits.

THEOPHRASTUS:

One ought to give her notice to reform her airs. She'd be less difficult to live with. Where does this change come from?

VALÈRE:

Why, it's because of her book.

THEPHRASTUS:

What! She's actually going to print it?

VALÈRE:

Yes.

THEOPHRSTUS:

If she's not put in order, they'll have to lock her up

DORTIDIUS:

Do you really grasp that, if need be, this act might suffice should you ever think of having her banished?

THEOPHRASTUS: (to Valère)

Are you familiar with her discourse on the duties if kings?

VALÈRE:

Ah, don't talk to me about it. I've reread it twenty times! It's necessary to endure this storm for now.

DORTIDIUS: (seriously)

Still, between ourselves, it's her best work. Do you think it's by her hand?

VALÈRE:

Right! You want to play a joke on me.

DORTIDIUS: (still serious)

No, on honor. It pleases me.

VALÈRE:

And you want to boast of it yourself!

DORTIDIUS:

I tell you it's fine. Why, very fine.

VALÈRE:

And you want to laugh. It's an absurdity bordering on delusion.

DORTIDIUS:

If I thought that of it, I would say it in whispers.

VALÈRE:

Get out! Your serious manner does not impose on me.

DORTIDIUS: (angrily)

Finally, sir. Make up your mind, and each must shut up.

VALÈRE:

Why, by the tone you are taking, I would think you are the father.

DORTIDIUS:

Well! If that were true?

VALÈRE:

My word. So much the worse for you.

DORTIDIUS: (more angry)

But my little gentleman—

VALÈRE:

I am in good faith.

DORTIDIUS:

It could come to some hard truths.

VALÈRE:

It always comes to insults when one is wrong.

DORTIDIUS:

You are pushing me past all bounds!

VALÈRE:

And what's more, I laugh about it.

DORTIDIUS: (furious)

Ah, that's too much!

THEOPHRASTUS:

Hey, gentlemen, if you please—

DORTIDIUS:

Pleasant joker—for me to run through.

THEOPHRASTUS: (stepping between them)

Gentlemen, let's not imitate Molière's pedants. Permit me, both of you, to put you in agreement.

VALÈRE:

As for me, I am right.

THEOPHRASTUS: (to Valère)

No question.

DORTIDIUS:

As for me, I am not wrong.

THEOPHRASTUS: (to Dortidius)

Truly, no. But still, someone might hear you and Cydalise might have surprised us already.

DORTIDIUS:

Esteem, which must always animate us—

THEOPHRASTUS:

It's not a question of esteem. We all know each other. But at least, come prudence. We want to keep up the appearance of friendship. It's through that beautiful façade that we impose; and we'll be ruined if we are divided. It's really necessary to let certain bagatelles pass. Hold on. They're coming to us. Forget your quarrels.

CYDALISE: (entering, book in hand)

Pardon, if I am late. I was occupied with you, and these are always my sweetest moments. Let's sit down, gentlemen. Ah, you are there, Valère? They've just brought me the proposal from my notary. You will be satisfied.

VALÈRE:

Madame, you know, my dearest wish in forming these beautiful ties, is to reaffirm the friendship that links us.

CYDALISE:

I owe you this happiness that's spreading through my life, and I am going to acquit myself towards you. But gentlemen, just now you were speaking heatedly. What important subject could divide you? At least, I thought I heard you arguing.

VALÈRE: (a little embarrassed)

It's true.

CYDALISE:

Might I know what you were descanting about with so much interest?

VALÈRE:

Since one must confess it, you were the object.

CYDALISE:

Me?

VALÈRE:

You. This warmth is the proof.

CYDALISE:

What's it about then?

VALÈRE:

Ah, I cannot say more about it. I don't know how to praise in the presence of people. Speak, gentlemen, speak!

THEOPHRASTUS:

You permit?

VALÈRE:

I consent to it.

THEOPHRASTUS:

We were searching through past centuries for a genius

to compare to you. I cited Aspasia; this gentleman was angered by the comparison.

VALÈRE:

I find it shocking, and here's my reason: in former times Aspasia could shine in Athens, but philosophy was hardly flourishing there. All nations, struck by its new brilliance, endured prostrating themselves before its cradle. All were, at that time, surprised. Ordinary talents shone better in the bloom in those vulgar centuries. But in our day, the mind has made so much progress, it's difficult after so much success to put oneself on the same level of the celebrated men whose shadow caused barbarism to flee. So that I cannot suffer, without putting myself in a rage, to judge between you and Aspasia. (to Theophrastus) Compare then these times and see where you go.

THEOPHRASTUS:

But comparisons are not perfect.

VALÈRE:

Come on, you were wrong.

THEPHRASTUS:

I feel it, and blush for it.

CYDALISE:

Don't go so far as to ask my opinion. I know too much.

VALÈRE: (with a tone of truthfulness)

We know that you are sublime.

DORTIDIUS:

These are our feelings. But how he expresses them! He knows how to embellish.

CYDALISE: (excitedly)

Ah, that's the truth.

VALÈRE: (kissing her hand)

Will you pardon me for this vivacity?

CYDALISE:

I ought to scold you. Your wit disarms me. I cannot hold to it. I am under a spell.

DORTIDIUS:

No one knows better how to be interesting.

VALÈRE: (to Dortidius)

I see that genius is still indulgent.

CYDALISE:

Mr. Dortidius, tell us some news.

DORTIDIUS:

I don't bother myself with bugs or their quarrels. What is the success of a siege or a battle to me? I leave affairs of state to our idlers. I trouble myself very little about the country I occupy. The true philosopher is a cosmopolitan.

CYDALISE:

One clings to the fatherland, that's the only link.

DORTIDIUS:

Fie! That's to limit oneself to being a citizen. The philosopher lives by himself in profound peace, far from the great dreamers who desolate the world. He turns away from these objects of honor. He is his own monarch and legislator. Nothing can alter the happiness of his being. It's up to the great ones to calm the troubles they create.

THEOPHRASTUS:

He looks into philosophy and sees it as it ought to be.

CYDALISE:

One never finds his wit wanting.

VALÈRE:

Madame, he's right. The philosophic spirit ought not to stoop to politics. These wars, these treaties, all these unimportant things are thrusting themselves, bit by bit, into the abyss of time. All this will disappear in the flames of genius. And, if one can speak without false modesty, except for you and us, I am unable to discover who will be the object of an honest conversation.

CYDALISE:

Yes, truly, they are wretches.

THEOPHRASTUD:

Who must be abandoned to vulgar wits.

CYDALISE:

That, by your authority, I shall not name. By the way: are they talking about some novelty?

VALÈRE:

We are planning only one.

CYDALISE:

A major work, doubtless.

VALÈRE:

It's a discovery; a new way that one undertakes to track a genre where genius can exercise itself?

CYDALISE:

A tragedy?

VALÈRE:

Yes, purely domestic—as we wish.

CYDALISE:

I'd be afraid of criticism. It's always against novelties. And the public

VALÈRE:

Truly, the public will decide like geese. We know that well enough. But, we'll make war.

CYDALISE:

I don't know. Old-fashioned taste still rules the stage.

VALÈRE:

It's true, we are risking, especially in the opening days. But we'll make an uproar to deafen them. We have friends who live in the theatre boxes, who are going to shout "Miracle!" and force them to praise us. Anyway, we will have a great success.

CYDALISE:

Yes, I wasn't thinking of that and you undeceived me.

VALÈRE:

We have so many people who devote themselves to us. So many small, tiny authors who, from pride, praise us, that I am assured with a little incense we can make them abjure good sense.

THEOPHRASTUS: (laughing)

Ha, ha, ha, ha, ha, ha. That's pure truth.

CYDALISE:

And will we have to wait a long while for this major work?

VALÈRE:

We are occupied with more important concerns.

CYDALISE:

Which are?

VALÈRE:

A certain author wants to represent us in a comedy.

CYDALISE:

That's a bold undertaking.

DORTIDIUS: (with fire)

Represent us! Why really, that's a crime of state! Represent us!

VALÈRE:

We know how to parry this outrage.

CYDALISE:

Ah, the entire public—

DORTIDIUS:

We might mistake ourselves. We have been badly drawn if he's going to render us.

CYDALISE:

The magistrates will raise their voice in one body.

THEOPHRASTUS:

We will throw these men of laws into confusion.

CYDALISE:

But the court—

VALÈRE:

—Will never take up our quarrel. We've acted cleverly with it.

THEOPHRASTUS:

You will see: it will be necessary to say a word to the author.

DORTIDIUS:

Yes, at least we could terrify him, if he can be frightened.

VALÈRE:

The worst part, gentlemen, is awaiting the storm. Until then, let's defame the author and the work. To avenge ourselves on him, let's arm the hands of fools. By employing others, we will strike more sure blows. Can't we win over the actors and the actresses? We will have a band right on stage. The cabal must excite rumor to point to us, even into the eyes of spectators in the boxes. I know the public. We have only to appear. It fears us.

CYDALISE:

That's well said, and he who braves it is its master. But our colporteur is really slow coming. He ought to be here. What can be keeping him?

DORTIDIUS:

Perhaps he's downstairs.

CYDALISE:

That's what I suspect. Hey, someone.

LACKEY: (appearing)

Madame?

CYDALISE:

Hasn't anyone come with books?

LACKEY:

No one.

CYDALISE: (with an uneasy gesture)

A secret order. Could he have been arrested? Call

Valentine.

LACKEY:

Madame, he's very ill and they fear for his life.

DORTIDIUS:

So much the better. He'll be a subject for our anatomy class.

CYDALISE:

But is he really so ill?

LACKEY:

He is desperate, Madame, and I take him for a buried man.

DORTIDIUS:

Poor Valentine! He's a lad that I love. And I'll keep him to dissect myself. (to Cydalise) But I think you ought to begin your course, Madame, because you still delay it.

CYDALISE:

For my part, that project was only a caprice.

LACKEY:

Here's the Colporteur.

(exit Lackey)

(Enter Propice)

CYDALISE:

Come in, Mr. Propice. Have you some new things?

PROPICE:

I'm not seeking for 'em. Madame, have you read "The Indiscreet Family Jewels"? It's philosophic enough. At least that's what they say.

CYDALISE:

The idea of it is funny, but no longer new.

PROPICE:

That still sells.

CYDALISE:

Pass that.

PROPICE:

Do you know "The Letter to the Deaf"?

CYDALISE:

The author presented it to me.

DORTIDIUS:

All his merit shines in that.

PROPICE:

You won't like "The Father of The Family." It's not very good.

DORTIDIUS: (ironically)

You'd know about that.

PROPICE:

But the public says so, and I believe it well enough. As to "The Book of Morals," I recall having sold it to you, Madame. (reading the titles) "Reflections on the Soul."

CYDALISE:

Let's see. I know it. Is that all?

PROPICE:

Actually, no. "The Interpretation of Nature."

CYDALISE:

Good! That's an excellent book.

DORTIDIUS:

Sublime.

THEOPHRASTUS:

Necessary.

CYDALISE:

I'll take it. Someone took my copy.

PROPICE:

This one. This is: "The Discourse on Inequality" by Rousseau.

CYDALISE: (taking it)

Ah, I am going to reread it avidly. What's that other writing there that I see?

PROPICE:

Madame, it's nothing. It's "The Little Prophet" by Grimm.

CYDALISE:

Ah! Ah! I recall. It's very amusing.

PROPICE:

Yes, it's a very pleasant jest. Are you wanting anything more from my little service?

CYDALISE:

No, I'm keeping this one. Good day, Mr. Propice.

(exit Propice) Ah, we'll reread my favorite book.

VALÈRE:

What! "Inequality"? It's mine, also.

THEOPHRASTUS:

That book is a treasure. It reduces all men to the rank of animals, and that's what we are. Man has made himself a slave by giving himself laws. And everything would go better if he lived in the woods.

CYDALISE:

As for me, I would experience a pure, voluptuous delight to see us all return to a state of nature.

THEOPHRASTUS:

Minds in error are still deeply plunged in it, and it retains them through so many prejudices. It's a wonder that many savants have not been choked by it.

CYDALISE:

But what do you want with us, Marton?

MARTON: (entering)

Madame, a philosopher is asking to speak with you.

CYDALISE:

What's his name?

MARTON:

Crispin.

CYDALISE:

That name is singular.

DORTIDIUS:

Yes, by God.

CYDALISE:

But, after all, names prove nothing. Ah, heavens, what

a surprise!

CRISPIN: (entering on all fours)

Madame, nothing offends me. I no longer dispute opinions. And it's the happy fruit of my philosophy which bows to all. It makes me choose the condition of a quadruped. On these four pillars, my body is better supported. And I see fewer fools who would wound my eyes.

CYDALISE: (to Valère)

He's an original in his system at least.

VALÈRE:

Why, he's very pleasant.

MARTON:

As for me, I feel that I love him.

CRISPIN:

By civilizing ourselves, we've lost everything: Health, Happiness, and every virtue. Therefore, I am returning myself to life of an animal. You see my kitchen, it's simple and frugal. (pulling out lettuce from his pocket) It is true, one cannot be content with less. But I know how to enrich myself by doing away with needs. Before that, fortune appeared to me to be unjust, and now I've become happier and more robust than all those courtiers in unmanning luxury—about which women still know the price. Forewarned of the reception you give to savants, Madame, I came to render you my homage; and to invite these gentlemen, perhaps, to imitate me. At least, if my example has what it takes to tempt them—

CYDALISE:

Do you know: that shows wit despite his folly.

DORTIFIUS:

Why, much.

MARTON:

I would say genius. And never has philosophy pleased me to such a degree.

THEOPHRASTUS:

This is what we've been looking for. A man convinced, full of his system, who braves criticism joining practice to speculation.

CYDALISE:

At bottom, this would be a man to respect, but because of prejudices one feels oneself checked.

CRISPIN:

My determination may seem bizarre to you—

CYDALISE:

You give to plain-speaking an example that is indeed rare. But your eagerness can only be flattering. You are a philosopher in the strict sense.

CRISPIN:

I forbid myself to consult fashion. I thought that clothes ought to be simple and nothing more. Even in a really hot climate.

THEOPHRASTUS:

Sire, here we judge a man by what he's worth, not by his clothes.

CRISPIN:

That's truly a wise way of thinking.

CYDALISE:

But who can be coming to us?

CARONDAS: (entering and staring at Crispin with embarrassment)

I've completed my message, Madame. And the Notary will arrive momentarily.

CYDALISE:

What's the matter with you?

CARONDAS: (pointing to Crispin who is hiding behind Cydalise)

Who is this pleasing animal?

CYDALISE:

He's a great philosopher; he'll be at the party.

CRISPIN:

In truth, Madame.

CARONDAS: (to Valère)

Ah, the cursed beast. We are discovered.

VALÈRE:

How's that?

CARONDAS:

It's Crispin, Damis' valet.

CRISPIN: (jumping up)

Eh, yes, Mr. Frontin. Speak louder. Yes, it's me.

CYDALISE:

What's this mystery all about?

CRISPIN: (pointing Valère out to Cydalise)

This gentleman's valet is your secretary. And I employed this disguise to place in your hands an important letter. (pointing to Carondas) Surprised at the home of this cheat!

CYDALISE:

I know the handwriting. (to Valère) It's yours, sir.

CRISPIN:

Read it, I conjure you.

VALÈRE: (to the philosophers)

Ah, we are ruined.

CYDALISE: (reading in an altered voice which weakens little by little)

"My dear Frontin, I am sending you this collection of impertinences that Cydalise refers to as her book. Continue to flatter this mad woman, who is imposed on by your name as a savant. Theophrastus and Dortidius have just communicated an excellent plan to me which will succeed in turning her head, and for which you will be necessary. Her nonsense, her oddities, her—"

CRISPIN:

She's lowering her voice and she won't go any further the way I see it.

CARONDAS:

Ah, traitor of a Crispin.

DORTIDIUS: (to Valère)

The adventure is vexing, but we are done with it.

VALÈRE: (low)

What a frightful disgrace. What to say to her? Let's leave.

CYDALISE:

Read, sir, read. And justify yourself if you dare. Indeed,

I was the victim of your seductions. And my eyes have opened at the edge of the abyss. What have I done to you for you to dare to treat me so? Go, and never reappear here in your life. Your confusion suffices for my vengeance. Ingrates! Perhaps, others will have less indulgence. That's the last hope of my outraged heart. Leave!

VALÈRE: (furious)

Ah! Wretch.

CARONDAS:

That's our dismissal.

(The philosophers leave)

CYDALISE:

The cruel creatures. To what degree they tricked me. Come, Damis, come. I feel that the sight of you reminds me of my blind intemperance.

DAMIS:

They are unmasked. Eros has only a moment. They are punished enough by no longer being feared. And you, Madame, need no longer complain of them.

CYDALISE:

I had sacrificed my most holy duties to those perverse men, and even friendship. Indeed, you are all avenged. My darling Rosalie, I recognize my wrongs. May your heart forget them. I will repair them all by giving you Damis.

DAMIS:

You will find the feelings of a son in me.

ROSALIE:

All my wishes are fulfilled. Heaven has given me my mother back.

CRISPIN:

As for me, to end the affair, I'm marrying Marton.

MARTON:

(to the public) We've pointed out the features of the sages of our time. We unmask the false, let us respect the true.

CURTAIN

THE STUMBLING BLOCK OF MORALS

CAST OF CHARACTERS

HONORÉ

LYSIMON, a relative and friend of Honoré

SOPHANES, a false philosopher[2]

MONDOR, financier and man of pleasure

ROSALIE

CLORINDE

ERMINIE

MARTON, Rosalie's servant

THE ABBÉ FICHET

A COACHMAN

A LACKEY

---

2. Palissot is attacking Diderot under the name Sophanes. In French this has the connotation of Wise-donkey. Palissot also attacked Diderot in another play, the one for which he remains famous, *Les Philosophes* (*The Philosophers*), which is included as the first half of this book.

ACT I

The Action takes place in Paris.

ROSALIE:

(busy considering different fabrics) Leave me alone to contemplate these new fabrics. What vanity! How beautiful the colors are.

MARTON:

Well, at last you are rejoicing in my advice! Are you repenting of having followed it? You are going to eclipse our proudest beauties.

ROSALIE:

This Peking ought to be admirable in the light.

MARTON:

(showing her a jewel box) This is worth a bit more. Look at these jewels. There, by Jove, solid presents—that can be changed into hard cash. Long live such works!

ROSALIE:

This hat enchants me. How it must embellish me! Quick, a mirror, Marton. I want to try it.

MARTON:

Let the chiffon be.

ROSALIE:

My word, the celebrated Bertin has been outdone. Look at this gracefully twined feather. What a success I'm going to have at the Opera Ball.

MARTON:

I recognize my sex in these stupidities. At bottom, this taste for luxury is not blameworthy. But the time's come to join utility with pleasantness. It's time to think. See this gold, which certainly comes from Mondor the financier. Its shape is antique and perhaps awkward; and as for me, I'd give all these fashionable chiffons for such a jewel.

ROSALIE:

Well, I'll make you a gift of it. This Mondor is so sad and of such a bad tone.

MARTON:

You could show him a little complaisance.

ROSALIE:

No. I am doing myself violence to endure him. And I cannot suffice to the boring proposals, that he constantly holds me in. With his diamonds, whose collection dazzles and intoxicates him, it's becoming more difficult to live each day; then there's his English hair which he curls at home. But he isn't coming to bring me his boredom.

MARTON:

Are you still burning to have a carriage? Well, if he offered it to you—would you have the courage to refuse to let him be one of your friends?

ROSALIE:

That would be paying dearly for it in my opinion.

MARTON:

Believe me—you must renounce this delicacy. You join to your allures the flower of your youth. Try to profit from it. But for your own good, realize that Mondor is a man enjoying favor, an essential man! His clever politics has taught him to make himself useful to the passions of the great. On that head alone he must be kept.

ROSALIE:

Does he think he can raise himself by such employment?

MARTON:

Does he think it? Why, no question. Are you still unaware that in this century the caduceus honored is the one that is sure to become everything. And that no condition is better greeted by all. It's a favorable act, and reduced to a system by more than one important person, by more even than the Abbé. Know our morals and disabuse yourself. Don't you notice they respect us? In the event one is pretty, are ancestors needed? France, by degrees, has polished itself to such a point that we give tone to the town, to the court. And all is pardoned to errors of love. Be confident on that score by my experience. The one that sees you today with indifference, will tomorrow, perhaps, place all his pride in receiving a glance from you.

ROSALIE:

You're recounting a romance to me.

MARTON:

A romance? No, my darling; Do you have less attractions than Naïs and Glycera? You've been able to observe them. Of their obscure origins the world hardly retains a confused memory. They are unaware in what places their youth was spent. Well, one's a Marquise and the other's a Viscountess.

ROSALIE:

What! They can forget themselves to this degree?

MARTON:

Surely. Whatever injures pride is forgotten in a moment. So then, have a bit of confidence in yourself. I see at your chariot a man of finance. One of our Senators.

ROSALIE:

Ah! Don't tell me about him. A dandy in a gown has little appeal for me.

MARTON:

You've already known how to charm a Great Wit en titre. And for you he's already composed more than one epistle.

ROSALIE:

Yes, the conquest was rare. A blasé scribbler who goes about dragging a worn-out persiflage everywhere. I am unaware of what talents he boasts of his person—but as soon as he sings, the pleasure bores.

MARTON:

I have no more respect for his voice than you do. Still, you'll agree it's nice at your age. This glory must sometimes be inconvenient—to receive incense from a fashionable poet. But what seems to me to be more seducing to you is to have obtained the imposing suffrage, the advice, the friendship of great personages, one that philosophy has placed among the ranks of the sages. To serve these gentlemen is not done by half.

ROSALIE:

Don't tell me any more of his friend, Marton.

MARTON:

Of Honoré?

ROSALIE:

Doubtless.

MARTON:

Still, I understand you. And if I believe in Honoré—indeed, he has the appearance of a happy mortal—the fortunate conqueror who must enchain your heart to his destiny. Romantic—and that's what pleases your age group. It's through you that love had its first homage. His charming face must have tempted you.

And what he proposes to you rightfully flatters you. But with him, especially beware of being imprudent. And if possible, keep an indifferent soul.

ROSALIE:

Either I know myself badly, or in my heart it's merely a simple inclination that speaks in his favor. I admire his good faith; his inexperience; his love is so real, so full of confidence that he believes whatever I want, and makes it his own. This sentimental tone is new to me. For, without disguising from myself what belongs to his youth, without blinding myself—still, his respect interests me. Besides, you know he's master of his destiny, and that he can, indeed, freely dispose of his hand. One day he ought to enjoy the greatest ease. Would you, putting faith in an idle hope, counsel me, Marton, not to attach myself to a more substantial happiness that seems to seek me out?

MARTON:

You're so used to subjugating Honoré. In his presence you've conducted yourself with so much reserve and discretion that I have no doubt of your intention. Still, your dissipated and flighty temperament doesn't suit well with marriage. But employ your rights right up until that day and learn how to join prudence and love.— You owe Mondor some gratitude.

ROSALIE:

Peace, Marton. Someone's coming. It's Honoré's friend.

(Enter Sophanes.)

SOPHANES:

Well! My Rosalie, finally the day has come, prepared for by my efforts, escorted by love, in which our destinies are going to assume a new face. I don't know if Honoré has lost his head, but I can depict ill his petulant ardor towards you; he comes from cajoling you to complete his happiness. To excite him further, I've disputed his idea: he doesn't listen to me. His head is determined. And never has passion shown such vigor. I leave to you the care of increasing it further. You can now dress in homespun. I will answer for success.

ROSALIE:

Why, my dear Philosopher, can you answer fully for me? We're to be reborn in his heart. If he came to blush? If the public? Custom—?

SOPHANES:

Custom, as you know, is the scorn of the sage. We've convinced him. Our purest feelings—aren't they always the work of our senses? Why seek a chimeric happiness elsewhere? Morality is only a word. We cling to the physical. You are pleasing to Honoré. Well, everything's for the best. Love had its end in mind when it created your eyes. What can you lack with the gift of pleasing? What reproach could Honoré make to you? You couldn't have reached the age I see you at without being permitted some attempt of your rights. I like your embarrassment. Why do you forbid it to yourself? You are reproaching yourself for a feeling and a tender heart? Only a misanthrope in his gloomy leisure makes a virtue of scoffing at pleasure. As for me, I sympathize with human weakness; and Ninon to my liking beats Lucretia.

ROSALIE:

Ah! Mr. Sophanes, are you flattering me?

SOPHANES:

Not I. I say what I think. Ask Marton.

MARTON:

My word, at least this morality is very useful.

SOPHANES:

Natural instinct is my rule and my code. I don't bow to those base scruples which rock the cradle of common humans. And I leave to pedants those austere precepts that put crime and weakness out of the nest.

ROSALIE:

Indeed, but does Honoré think as you? And suppose he came to change?

SOPHANES:

No, he's too jealous of appearing free of vulgar prejudices ever to revert to these popular errors. You can really be confident of me, anyway. (in a low voice) Between ourselves, you know what I owe you. My favorite virtue is gratitude. And I think I've acquitted myself of it by delivering Honoré to you.

ROSALIE:

Well! I'm abandoning myself to your advice.

SOPHANES:

By Jove! What can you risk with such a nice wager? Honoré, in the heat of his amorous excitement, thinks you're from an honest and unfortunate family. Expressly for you, Love is loaning him its blindfold. And the more his mania is to see everything as perfect. Only, let Marton flatter him and second you. This Marton's got all the good sense in the world. By the way, it's time to use the supposed letter from Milord Calenfort. (fumbling in his pockets) I think I have it on me. Marton will prudently choose the time to regale Honoré with it. Why—what? Could I have lost it? No, here it is. (gives letter to Marton) Goodbye. I don't want him to meet me here.

(Exit Sophanes.)

ROSALIE:

This Mr. Sophanes is an excellent soul.

MARTON:

Yes, his philosophy is completely laughable.

ROSALIE:

He spares nothing to serve his friends. He's full of heat.

MARTON:

Truly, that's plain to see. His morality. My word, he predicted correctly. Honoré is coming to us. Put on your august manner.

(Enter Honoré.)

HONORÉ:

Dear Rosalie, you owe it to yourself to relax your reserve towards me. I have some right, at least, to your confidence. To what additional proof will you put my constancy? Who would think that with such soft eyes you are so barbarous?

ROSALIE:

But what wrong have I done? Of what do you complain?

HONORÉ:

(with fire) I complain—I complain to see you indecisive. Is this the friendship you promised me? I want to avenge the unjust fate that rendered Fortune blind in your regard. It's my dearest wish. Cruel adversity in my tender eyes makes you more beautiful. Still, pardon the pressing interest which inspires in me a sympathetic heart for you, and perhaps interested me to excess in your charms. If I believe there are secret alarms in this heart, you have pains you've disguised from me. Could you have relatives exposed to wrongs? I offer you my credit, my services for them.

ROSALIE:

(with considerable dignity) No, fate has kept all its injustices for me. But if my only share was obscurity, if it has placed so much inequality between us, ought I to permit you to have the least hope? Who, me? To swallow you? What are you thinking, Honoré?

HONORÉ:

Eh! Why hesitate to receive my hand? What odious caprice—

ROSALIE:

You are urging me in vain.

HONORÉ:

Ah, you hate me and all my tenderness.

ROSALIE:

(in the most august tone) Honoré, in abusing so much delicacy, I am not insensible of love. But I intend to force you to esteem me one day by combating the error by which your soul is seduced. You see to what fate fortune has reduced me. I cannot without terror suppose the moment when your eyes, well forewarned by me, suddenly light up, seeing the precipice toward which an amorous caprice is leading you. Think, when I refuse a role so sweet that perhaps I am more to be pitied than you. Like your love, my weakness is extreme. But, if possible, I mean to save you from yourself.

MARTON:

(low to Rosalie) Marvelous!

HONORÉ:

Cease these superfluous efforts. Learn that my heart is no longer its own. You are reproaching yourself too much for errors of youth that no longer abase your noble soul. Misfortune ought not to inspire remorse. And fortune still wants to repair its wrong. You love me. Ah, deign to say it to me again a hundred times. All these vain prejudices whose power I brave, and that you oppose to me with so much rigor—won't prevent me from recognizing my happiness. Come!

ROSALIE:

You wish it. Well, my dear Honoré— Why, no. I fear the violence of your love. Try, at least, to moderate its fire and give yourself time to test it a little. Wait, this evening at my home, you will have company. I promised you Clorinde and the young Erminie. What am I doing? Gayety, dissipation, could somewhat divert your fires. You will have need of them. You will come, I hope.

HONORÉ:

What won't I do in my ardor to please you? But my heart, in its turn, imposes a rule on you.

ROSALIE:

Which is?

HONORÉ:

That at least tomorrow you will accept my faith.

ROSALIE:

(to Marton) How pressing you are! Got to satisfy him. (to Honoré) Tomorrow—so be it! I am leaving for a moment on business.

MARTON:

(low to Rosalie) You're going to Mondor's?

ROSALIE:

(low to Marton) Got to. (to Honoré, aloud) Goodbye.

(Rosalie leaves.)

HONORÉ:

At last, I've the happiness of obtaining her confession. But my dear Marton, you, who read in my soul—from whence comes this frigidity which is unworthy of my flame? I thought I noticed a certain embarrassment in her. Really, does she love me?

MARTON:

Ah! You cannot suspect it. Never has the eye of love been able to mistake itself. This timid embarrassment is easy to understand. She loves you and fears, by accepting your wishes, to abase you, despite yourself, to the power of her eyes.

HONORÉ:

She complains so often of the wrongs of fortune. My curiosity may seem importunate. But I will return to it still. You know all her secrets—of relatives she supports and, perhaps, indiscreet— Don't they abuse her fond kindness?

MARTON:

Why should she make up a useless mystery to you? It's true, her family is not in splendor. Without opulence, they can be far from misfortune. Ah! You know Rosalie's heart. Without wanting to boast, nor believing it accomplished, sir, you will discover great ingenuity in it.

HONORÉ:

I believe it. Her portrait can only be flattering.

MARTON:

I'd still like to see her more prudent. And that she were less indolent about her fortune. But I don't have the gift of persuading her. Sir, it's on that topic she must be scolded. And not her coldness, which is apparent. If you knew the seductive offer she sacrificed to you—

HONORÉ:

To me, Marton?

MARTON:

For you. But her heart is too jealous of such secrets. I must respect it.

HONORÉ:

Mercy.

MARTON:

I promised my mistress to keep silent. Oh, no weakness.

HONORÉ:

Can you suspect me, dear Marton? Let yourself be disarmed.

MARTON:

Ah, my heart is too good. (gives him a letter) Here, sir, read. Judge if she loves you. And if you are not extremely unjust, see what is being refused. Well? Am I wrong?

HONORÉ:

(reading the end of the letter) "The fortune and the hand of Lord Calenfort."

MARTON:

Alas, he left for London in despair.

HONORÉ:

So noble a proceeding justly confuses me! In a humble fortune, o heaven! How much grandeur! You don't astonish me; I've read in her heart. And yet I am going to dry the murmurings, the bitter reproaches, perhaps the insults of a crowd of fools, whose importunate voices are soon going to rise in condemnation of my choice. I admire extremely human inconsequentiality! Do you believe it, madam? Even Mr. Sophanes, whom I've seen combat with so much vigor the rigidity of public prejudices a hundred times, opposed this vain tyranny against me this morning and seemed, for me alone, to give the lie to his genius.

MARTON:

What! Mr. Sophanes?

HONORÉ:

I made him blush for it. But what a difference there is between talking and acting. At least you will see me display more courage in creating my happiness despite custom. But, what can be bringing my relative, Lysimon? From whence is he coming here? Withdraw, Marton.

(Marton leaves.)

LYSIMON:

(entering) My dear, Honoré, I've learned strange news. Must I displease you in proving my zeal? Friendship forbids me to disguise anything from you. If I believe the public, you are going to marry a girl without name, and that your seduced soul apparently is unaware of her morals and her conduct. From whence proceeds this suspicion with which you are besmirched? I learned from Sophanes that you were here. And I flew to you without losing a moment. Wounded honor inspires all that is in me in such a situation. How has this injurious rumor spread?

HONORÉ:

I respect the bonds of our attachment, Lysimon; you respect Rosalie's heart. Often one is deceived in all that the public knows of my heart—which sees nothing in itself to reproach itself for, nor to reveal, nor to hide from you. Nor reason to consult common opinion. Far from ambition, master of my fortune, I intend, it's true, to dispose of my faith. Henceforth it no longer exists except for me.

LYSIMON:

Now that's where philosophy is leading you; by abusing thought, it glorifies itself, the better to be able to brave morality.

HONORÉ:

Philosophy only makes war on unjust errors.

LYSIMON:

You can pride yourself on heroic courage by renouncing public esteem for yourself. But the fruits of the marriage that you are contemplating, victims of the scorn you affect here, will be condemned to blush at the mere name of their mother, and be punished by their birth for the weakness of a father. Will they have, at need, this odious courage?

HONORÉ:

Lysimon, I'll take care to open their eyes against the prejudices that incense the vulgar. Let's discontinue a conversation that's offensive to friendship. You are speaking of an object that is foreign to you. You must know her before judging her. You know what poison slander spreads. You yourself would blush, in seeing Rosalie, for having lent your ear to such imposture if you knew her heart.

LYSIMON:

Since the public voice has condemned her morals. I won't see her without some repugnance, except to prevent misfortune to Honoré.

HONORÉ:

What! Not even want to be disabused? Your eyes—

LYSIMON:

I don't think that would have injured me. I am disinterested and love is distracting you.

HONORÉ:

No, since I honor in this case the rarest virtue. Believe that to love alone I am not proud. Rosalie, to my eyes, without wealth and without attractions, would still have qualities that please me. (showing him the letter from Calenfort) Judge if this refusal is that of a vulgar soul. Weigh this procedure.

LYSIMON:

(after having read) You believe that? Why, the first talent of these tricky ladies is to dare, at need, to forge these titles for themselves. I only wish that your eyes be opened. And that I could prove to you—

HONORÉ:

You can't prove anything to me.

LYSIMON:

I've known Calenfort. There must be a way, since he's

left, of obtaining a proof—allow there to be a test.

HONORÉ:

No, my dear Lysimon. Return that letter to me. If you please, let's terminate the discussion of this object. You may think me either fantastic or credulous— My choice may to you seem bizarre or ridiculous. I will consult only my heart on this matter. Goodbye.

(Honoré leaves.)

LYSIMON:

Let's try again to save him from his error. In all social ranks a blind license produces so much assurance in broad daylight! This guilty excess has lasted too long. And I would dare to expect a lucky change. The French have always followed the example of their Master. Everything invites me to think that morals are going to revive.

CURTAIN

ACT II

MARTON:

Love will be able to do it! It's speaking marvelously. But one time, at least, danger is awaiting you. Time presses; let's try to embroil them both. Or Honoré, in the end, might open his eyes.

ROSALIE:

This Mr. Lysimon is really so formidable then?

MARTON:

Oh, I'll answer for that. I think he's the devil that Hell detached specifically against us. To struggle against us and to interfere with our plan. I went on guard seeing him appear. And to parry the blows that he brought us in train, from this closet I found the way to listen right to the end of their annoying conversation. What an abominable man with such an austere face. I never experienced so much rage. And if he hadn't left just as I was about to burst, I don't know to what excess I might have been carried.

ROSALIE:

But how did Honoré react?

MARTON:

He was annoyed. A concentrated scorn that he had trouble controlling, and that his passion wanted to hide. He seemed at every word ready to exhale. Never has love had such empire over a mortal. It's a blindness that approaches delirium! But he must awaken. With a new effort they might conquer the strongest in his head, and banish the prestige wherein our hopes are founded. Have you, by chance, met this Mr. Lysimon in society?

ROSALIE:

Very little.

MARTON:

I appreciate that. But do you know him?

ROSALIE:

I've seen him sometimes.

MARTON:

That's enough. I intend—Honoré is so credulous! Yes, this expedient is not very ridiculous. Sophanes, at need, can prop him up again. It will succeed for us.— You've seen Mondor?

ROSALIE:

Yes, I've warned him of Honoré's plans, and he seemed flattered by this confidence.

MARTON:

And he approves your action?

ROSALIE:

But with conditions.

MARTON:

I'm listening.

ROSALIE:

He first of all seized the opportunity to send right away to inform Erminie, even Clorinde, so that nothing will take place in front of Honoré, through stupidity, that could cause some umbrage.

MARTON:

Very fine. Either I'm much deceived or this precaution, quite naturally, would have escaped you. For we have a spirit of frailty; a butterfly is not more flighty. Happily,

Mondor is always full of zeal. (looking attentively at Rosalie's hand) Why, what new diamond is sparkling on your fingers? It's of the most beautiful fire.

ROSALIE:

By the way, Marton, has my guitar instructor arrived?

MARTON:

Who? Your Abbé Fichet? What the devil are you doing with that gigolo? This is really the moment for it!

ROSALIE:

How strict you've become! Do you know that people dote on such a light voice! So well modulated, such brilliant timber. It's from him that Clorinde's taken a hankering for singing.

MARTON:

And it seems you are burning to be taught by him? What if Honoré comes?

ROSALIE:

You will make him wait. And it's also my day for drawing.

(Exit Rosalie.)

MARTON:

Truly painting is what we are lacking! Nice arrangement! Come on, although stupid, she has some fine whims, and in the end, I cannot place my services better. I am trumps at gambling; besides. a Lysimon must not beat Marton on credit. Here, very much apropos, I see Honoré coming.

HONORÉ:

(entering, to himself) What an excess of wildness, what extravagance. Marton, has your mistress returned?

MARTON:

Not yet.

HONORÉ:

How many moments stolen from love.

MARTON:

She cannot be late. You seem enraged, sir. Allow me to clarify a mystery. You see me again in an emotion.

HONORÉ:

What is it?

MARTON:

You wouldn't have had, you and this Lysimon—a quarrel?

HONORÉ:

Where's this apprehension come from? It surprises me.

MARTON:

Alas, my soul was very affected seeing him first. How very jealous he is—he used to have some great plans for us.

HONORÉ:

What—for Rosalie?

MARTON:

Eh, yes! Truly for her! I was trembling that he'd come to seek a quarrel with you. For between ourselves, he was so badly treated, and I've often seen an animosity that caused me a terrible fear for her.

HONORÉ:

What are you telling me, Marton? Is it credible?

MARTON:

What? Nothing is more certain. But what's stopped me is that up to now they didn't want you to be told. It's true, Rosalie rid herself of him so promptly, that he's hardly in her thoughts. But Mr. Sophanes ought to remember it.

HONORÉ:

Kiss me, my heart cannot contain itself.

MARTON:

Why's that?

HONORÉ:

If you knew with how much address he came to me to blacken your mistress, to reproach my choice, and my blindness. How he counterfeited the tone of feeling. Oh! I would defy you to prevent yourself from laughing.

MARTON:

On honor—it was he who came to tell you?

HONORÉ:

On honor!

MARTON:

Oh, my word. The deed is very amusing.

HONORÉ:

I never saw anything so diverting. But if I were to depict to you his prudish manner, his gravity, his arrogance, and his pedantry— (he laughs) You couldn't contain yourself. Well, let him be imposing with his great airs. I promise myself truly to take my revenge.

MARTON:

I would bring him a thrust less frank; oppose trick for trick, and without emotion, without losing my temper, without any explanation. I would, until the end, follow his perfidy. My word, I would stretch the comedy out until after your marriage.

HONORÉ:

That would be best. Well said, ha, ha, ha.

SOPHANES:

(entering) You are laughing with a good heart indeed? I came to denounce myself to you, dear Honoré, for having perhaps committed an extreme indiscretion by addressing this sad Lysimon to you.

MARTON:

(very hurriedly) You are accusing yourself justly. The mistreated rival whose jealousy approaches frenzy; for you know how his pride was injured, and how ardent he is, despite his glacial manner. By luck, his scorn is limited to insults.

SOPHANES:

Murmurs are permitted to unhappy love. (To Honoré) You must forgive him.

HONORÉ:

If he only offended me; but Rosalie?

SOPHANES:

Well, it ought to be one more triumph for you. At least nothing makes me prouder than a jealous rival. He really told you about it then?

HONORÉ:

I was unaware of his motive, but by Jove, vanity is indeed vindictive. It's a wild outburst against my marriage.

SOPHANES:

Indeed, I warned you. You have only the suffrage that

some wits have hardly noticed. And, yet, for certain, attacked by envy, you are doing what presently I thought you must be told. But by the sovereign empire of your reason, you are raised above the claims of the senseless mob which shrieks in the name of morality. Myself, blindly, I invite you to do it. Rosalie has wit, talent, looks. As an honest man, at least, I believe she has the virtues needed for happiness. What more do you need?

HONORÉ:

Ah! I recognize you by this noble language. What can prejudice accomplish against the voice of Wisdom!

MARTON:

My word. True happiness is to live for oneself.

SOPHANES:

Did you really know that Marton is a philosopher?

MARTON:

Me! All I know are the laws of nature. I would be so little bothered if the world murmured about it. As for the slanderers— But, someone is coming.

HONORÉ:

See if it's Rosalie.

MARTON:

Oh, yes, I hear her voice. I'm going!

SOPHANES:

Goodbye, my dear fellow. Certain duties of custom force me to leave you; but there's compensation for you of a very sweet sort.

(Sophanes notices Rosalie and greets her respectfully.)

HONORÉ:

Till tomorrow.

SOPHANES:

Surely.

(Exit Sophanes.)

HONORÉ:

His eyes will witness our engagement, charming Rosalie, and this faithful friend will make our union yet more solemn. He will be the guarantee of the vows of love.

ROSALIE:

For me, I wish to give you a guarantee in my turn,

which ought never to be less costly it seems to me. Look at this portrait. Do you find it resembles me?

MARTON:

I find it speaking.

HONORÉ:

It's indeed precious to me. But, pardon—my heart doesn't see your eyes there. Those eyes, so seducing, that love alone can make. Perhaps, in the artist, it is nothing to be found. I agree, the portrait is charming—but wait—there! Without prejudice, you yourself examine it. See if that mouth wherein reigns such a sweet smile here offers allures that cannot be described. That sweet freshness, this sensual tone. How unfruitful the efforts of art seem. To the glance of a lover it seems unfaithful! How much more touching and beautiful. I feel the entire price of a favor so dear.

ROSALIE:

They say you've got a story to tell me. Aren't you going to speak to me of Mr. Lysimon?

HONORÉ:

I would think you lacking in pronouncing his name. But mercy, pardon his extravagance. He's punished enough by your indifference.

ROSALIE:

(with cleverness) His speech didn't make an impression on you?

HONORÉ:

You can judge.

MARTON:

I think the acts of a jealous man are not made to give umbrage.

HONORÉ:

He wouldn't have inspired so much in me, if I had known of his secret feelings. Regretfully, he deprived me of my sweetest moments; but I am sacrificing them to my unique business. I've set up a meeting tonight at my notary's. It's your interests that we must regulate. And I still have some papers to put together. Goodbye.

ROSALIE:

Come back—we're having company.

HONORÉ:

I'll do it.

(Exit Honoré.)

MARTON:

That child loves you to madness and you owe him some tenderness in return.

ROSALIE:

In the end so much love must inspire love. I think that by degrees his passion is inflaming me. And it's no longer pride which commands my soul.

MARTON:

I think I hear someone.

ROSALIE:

It's Mondor, surely, who's bringing company. Quickly, arrange armchairs. (Rosalie runs to greet her friends) What! It's you.

(Clorinde, Erminie, and Mondor enter.)

CLORINDE:

We are running, my queen, to congratulate you on your coming grandeur!

MONDOR:

Is Honoré here?

ROSALIE:

No, but he'll return.

ERMINIE:

We had plans to go to the opera. But we preferred you to Chevalier Gluck. We've come to spend the evening with you.

ROSALIE:

Nothing is more obliging. Marton, show them in; and tell Marin to come light up the place. (to the company) Well! What news do you have to bring me?

CLORINDE:

They say that Arsinoe has just left Clitandre.

MONDOR:

What, truly?

CLORINDE:

Yes, truly, and the deed is really good. (to Rosalie) You know they were taken with a beautiful passion. It was mutual, at least in appearance, like loves of olden times, incredible constancy. They sequestered themselves from the world absolutely, and this is called a thunderbolt of love.

ROSALIE:

Well?

CLORINDE:

To make it short for you, one fine morning our august heroine took flight on the sly; the servants were seduced, the baggage carried off, the poor lover was sleeping in the faith of oaths. Judge of his awakening, when a fatal indicia made him see plainly that he'd lost his Eurydice.

ERMINIE:

(drawling plaintively) I lost my Eurydice.

ROSALIE:

He'll get her back without going to hell.

HORTENSE:

Why, truly they say he's been replaced.

ROSALIE":

What! Already?

MONDOR:

No question: Arsinoe was never vacant.

ERMINIE:

Her conduct, it is true, was always very prudent.

ROSALIE:

What do they say about Aglaea?

ERMINIE:

My word, the handsome Orval is running about with her; you cannot do much worse. He had carried her off from the Financier Chryasante, who had built her a charming house. He at least owed her compensation. He just left her pitilessly to take up with the celebrated Amelie at the Opera.

ROSALIE:

It seems to me Aglaea is a thousand times prettier.

ERMINIE:

She has beautiful hair.

CLORINDE:

But of a very pronounced blonde.

ROSALIE:

I'd never suspected it.

CLORINDE:

It's a fact nonetheless.

ROSALIE:

Her complexion—

MONDOR:

Has some dazzle thanks to the powder she uses.

ROSALIE:

Her?

MONDOR:

You only have to see her to judge.

ROSALIE:

Ah, that's slander.

MONDOR:

I tell you she uses it. If only she'd asked me the secret, I wouldn't have told it.

ERMINIE:

A more incredible fact. And between ourselves, I treated it as first as a fable— It's that Julie—

ROSALIE:

Well?

ERMINIE:

Oh, my word. Guess!

MONDOR:

I'm unable.

ROSALIE:

Nor can I.

ERMINIE:

Try, imagine.

CLORINDE:

Has she made yet another dupe?

ERMINIE:

Would I hold you in suspense for a bagatelle like that? She's become religious to the point of affecting remorse.

ROSALIE:

(bursting into laughter) Julie, remorseful?

MONDOR:

She's got the devil in her.

ERMINIE:

You're missing the point; the prude's getting married.

MONDOR:

Who is the mortal whose soul is so hardened—?

ERMINIE:

He's a sort of grouch, a noble country bumpkin—they say Mr. Nacquard.

ROSALIE:

Nacquard as much as you like; but despite her reform, her ignoble manners, and her enormous body, Julie is, in every respect, a revolting sight.

MONDOR:

Ah! Her eyes reveal that enough.

ROSALIE:

Yes, that's the only thing human she has about her.

ERMINIE:

For all that the news is not less certain.

CLORINDE:

May God preserve forever from all bad luck, the face, the august face, of good Mr. Nacquard.

ROSALIE:

You have nothing to tell me of the illustrious Arsenie?

MONDOR:

They pretend she's leading a sad enough life with her Commander. He's so jealous of her that no one can speak to her without throwing him into a rage. In all Paris they are the most somber duo. At performances, at balls, he follows her like a shadow, and doesn't perceive that she's providing him this supreme happiness that he's tasting in avenging himself.

CLORINDE:

What can keep her in this harsh slavery?

MONDOR:

Greed. He gives her a brilliant outfit. Diamonds without number, a train of the best fashion. And they even fight in more than one house. He's gambling to ruin himself, despite his opulence, and that is what Arsenie is prudently awaiting.

ROSALIE:

They say her sister is much happier.

ERMINIE:

Alceste, they say, is even more amorous.

ROSALIE:

At least she had good guarantees for her tenderness.

CLORINDE:

What do you mean?

ROSALIE:

He left the little Duchess, who, priding herself, for the first time on honor, purchased constancy, at least for the term of a month. They say she's furious, outré, inconsolable. At bottom, Alceste must be a man too good to be true, to occasion such lively sorrows.

ERMINIE:

They say he gains by the exchange?

ROSALIE:

Yes, on the side of morals.

MONDOR:

Still, for Cleone it's a very fine sacrifice.

ROSALIE:

No question, and very flattering for the daughter of a Swiss.

CLORINDE:

What! That's all she is!

ERMINIE:

Perhaps even less.

CLORINDE:

That ought to take her down a peg or two.

ROSALIE:

My word, the picture of our morals is really bizarre.

ERMINIE:

What! Reflections? That fantasy is rare. (singing offstage) What's that uproar mean? Is it a wedding song?

MONDOR:

Eh! It's Abbé Fichet in all his originality.

CLORINDE:

He is always found in good company.

ABBÉ:

(entering) Your two arias are noted, divine Rosalie. You have the first and the second.

MONDOR:

That's the way it's done!

ERMINIE:

What hardened eyes he has!

CLORINDE:

Who cares: he will teach us some new songs.

ABBÉ:

I always regret refusing the beauties. But indiscreetly, a month ago, I took too much punch which has scratched my voice. They are giving a superb party for Celainte. I have to sing and act a proverb. What's more maddening to me than a proverb! And honor bright, I am forced to be strict. One day I shall be the victim of my talent. And I am going, some time, to exile myself on a diet. I am annihilated.

ERMINIE:

What! Without remission?

ABBÉ:

What, me pray? That's my aversion.

ROSALIE:

Ah! Don't make an indiscreet demand on him. He needs—

ABBÉ:

I am going to risk an aria, since you force me to do it, but it's in secrecy. Celainte would never forgive me—

(He hums a bit and then sings a short aria.)

ROSALIE:

Delicious!

CLORINDE:

Inconceivable!

ERMINIE:

Unique!

MONDOR:

Profound harmony! Speaking of music, would you have plans for Vaux-Hall tonight?

ERMINIE:

(excitedly) Vaux-Hall is deserted; rather, let's go to the ball. Mondor will take us.

MONDOR:

No, I gave my word to go to the Marais for the lottery.

ROSALIE:

You couldn't miss this engagement?

MONDOR:

No, but for you I see another arrangement. You could dispose of my English coach.

ROSALIE:

Ah! You are charming!

MONDOR:

You will be comfortable in it. At need, the Abbé will stay with you. You shall have it in an hour.

ROSALIE:

Till much later, dear Mondor.

MONDOR:

You can count on it.

CLORINDE:

(to Rosalie) Eh! Why, charming queen, tell us a little about your august chain. Are you irredeemably going to take a husband?

MONDOR:

By Jove, this is a great day for you!

ERMINIE:

How are you managing this wretched Honoré? Is he still blind and full of confidence? Apparently we won't ruin you?

MONDOR:

Oh! No! (noticing Honoré) Why, it's himself.

CLORINDE:

(composing herself, and raising her voice so Honoré will hear it) They say he's of the best fashion. (to Honoré) Ah, we were speaking of you and, from the bottom of my soul, I was praising you to Madame.

ERMINIE:

Assuredly, it's evident you are a connoisseur, and you couldn't place your heart better.

CLORINDE:

Let's not rob them of moments full of charm. (low to Erminie) Tonight we must all put ourselves under arms. (to Rosalie) Mondor, let's take leave of Madame. Till later. We are going to rush to return sooner. (they leave)

ROSALIE:

You were indeed delayed?

HONORÉ:

I'm coming from my Notary; but one is never done with these men of business! Forgive me. This duty grasped my heart too much; I was very jealous to assure my happiness.

ROSALIE:

I thought I could count on your complaisance.

HONORÉ:

Ah, never doubt your claims on me.

ROSALIE:

They mentioned a ball which must be charming. There we could talk freely, by ourselves. This plan made me smile and I can no longer stop myself. Go change clothes and come back to take me.

CURTAIN

ACT III

ROSALIE:

Is my rouge on good, Marton?

MARTON:

Divinely.

ROSALIE:

I think this mole is placed artistically. How do you like me?

MARTON:

I find you charming, and the ball will not have a beauty more brilliant. Honoré, proudly enchained under your sway, will see all eyes applauding his choice. You are going to ignite a thousand flames in all hearts, charm all husbands, and desolate all wives.

ROSALIE:

Today I have no such pretension. And I am even

pondering—

MARTON:

What! Truly?

ROSALIE:

I was thinking that Clorinde, Erminie, are no longer suitable for me.

MARTON:

What craziness! You who cannot be without them for a moment!

ROSALIE:

Between ourselves, I find them a little indecent. In their eyes, loaded with jealousy, didn't you see the secret scorn with which their souls are seized? And I do not escape their sneering tones, their wanton remarks, their mocking smiles. Marrying Honoré, I must accustom myself henceforth to place an immense interval between that world and myself. To humiliate them, Marton, I intend to have a Swiss footman in rich livery, in the end a complete outfit that custom grants to women of my rank. And if by some chance I meet them, I shall make it my happiness to put them in despair.

MARTON:

That will be your situation; what could they say?

ROSALIE:

Ah! Nothing will contain the fury of their scorn. But that will be from a distance, and I won't hear their insolent remarks, their perfidious outbursts. Ah, Marton, what delight to crush rivals who believe themselves right in treating us as equals. How greatly I'm going to rejoice in their confusion.

MARTON:

Why, it's necessary to stand on one's rank. I much approve of you. Still, from prudence, dissimulate this desire for revenge until after your wedding.

ROSALIE:

Indeed, that's what I'm doing, and even forcing them to second my intentions. It's necessary to put a reign on their treacherous tongues, to squander the most tender caresses on them. They will lose nothing by it, and my feelings—

(Enter Sophanes.)

SOPHANES:

Well, all is prepared by your arrangement, my dear

Rosalie? Are you marrying Honoré? Beware of betraying yourself through some negligence. Lysimon may be hiding some bad plan, and I am informed he has some maneuver in hand.

ROSALIE:

What! Could he still give us some umbrage?

MARTON:

If it's necessary to struggle against a new storm, we will know how to put Señor Lysimon in the shadow. Haven't you got Love and Marton on your side. (pointing to Rosalie) And above all, what I am confiding myself to are those eyes, and Mr. Sophanes and his philosophy!

ROSALIE:

And Honoré, besides; could Honoré at this moment renounce his tender eagerness?

SOPHANES:

Sometimes a moment is not without consequences. Still, to speak truly, I see little sign of it. But if, in the end by mischance he came to change, there would really be not much to be afflicted over. At bottom, marriage is only a popular bond. A mere nothing.

MARTON:

Without a doubt. With his character marriage would never find grace in my eyes.

SOPHANES:

You could easily find yourself much better or worse as far as fortune goes in the age we are living in. Interest is the god that captivates men. In Paris everything depends on casting over one's name an imposing glaze of reputation, and everything is useful for that, even a little scandal. Hold on, I have for example a Treatise on Morality that I am just now ready to publish. My word, I am tempted to dedicate it to you. Suddenly, by means of this trick you will have the certificate of a great female wit, a club, a tribunal, an accredited name. That's the way we use celebrity. Amongst us there's no slender genius, no author so little celebrated that he lacks his Aspasia. I'll put you in the secret. In such a role, at need, you might succeed, and it will take you very far. Confide yourself to my zeal, to my experience. Besides, it's not certain that you will lose Honoré.

ROSALIE:

Be it love, be it pride, I cling to this romantic novel.

MARTON:

By Jove! I cling to it also; I carried out the plan of it, and I've known how to dispose of Honoré in a way that he ought to get in a fight with Lysimon. (to Rosalie) Go, I predict for you the most delightful success. But, with the concurrence of Mr. Sophanes, you must think of dressing quickly, Madame. That's one way the more for our success. Tonight we will have Honoré under hand. We will lead him to the ball and finish him off tomorrow.

(Exit Rosalie and Marton.)

SOPHANES:

(alone) As of now, Rosalie is very sterile goods, but one day her beauty might make her useful. Got to manage her. You never know what you can do with such a pretty face.

(Enter Honoré.)

SOPHANES:

Ah, there you are, Honoré, garbed as a conqueror. It's apparent that you are preparing a celebration for Love. It's still for tomorrow?

HONORÉ:

Yes, that's the happy day that's going to deliver Rosalie

to my wishes. Nothing can equal my tender impatience. Why, what! It's Lysimon.

(Enter Lysimon.)

LYSIMON:

I see, my dear Honoré, that you weren't expecting my importunate return. You are counting the moments that I stole from love. But I've just completed some necessary courses which could give you important light. You thought my mind was rather preoccupied: indeed, false rumors could have deceived me. One is so trusting when one is in love, anyway. But I had to come right here immediately. With facts really conflated, very certain, very plain. You owe yourself these enlightenments, at least. I am awaiting them, I tell you, and you are going to learn the destiny, which, but for me, threatens you. My resource is still in the depth of your heart. Consult it: it was born for honor, Honoré.

HONORÉ:

Lysimon, you could spare yourself these efforts; I've already told you, your proceedings are in vain. Besides, I know their motives, and that's enough. But to spare you so many ill-placed cares, I am marrying Rosalie. Do not outrage any further a name that is allied to mine. (ironically) I won't urge you to be a witness. I see you could get carried away too far.

LYSIMON:

Don't you blush at such an alliance? (to Sophanes) How is it you suffer it, you the friend of Honoré, you that I am surprised to meet here, you Mr. Sophanes?

SOPHANES:

(in a light-hearted tone) He is really hardened. I attempted, like you to combat his passion. But all my morality slid off his soul. To speech that soon I couldn't control; he himself must think me a prejudiced man. Indeed, I know that people will blame his mania. But indiscreet zeal becomes tyranny. Besides, even friendship has its bias. The happy, as you know, cling to their opinions. He is braving all inconvenient custom. Each has the right to be happy after his own fashion.

LYSIMON:

O Heaven! With what stumbling blocks he is surrounded. How the name of friend seems profaned to me! Eh, what vile flatterers by their culpable cleverness always lead imprudent youth astray.

HONORÉ:

My heart grasps the entire worth of this moral jargon. Still, between ourselves, I am not surprised that it was sometimes capable of wearying Rosalie.

LYSIMON:

Wearying her? Who? Me? What is this folly, Honoré?

SOPHANES:

(to Honoré) You will see that he doesn't know her.

HONORÉ:

You act wondrously, and the air of embarrassment is very comic, at least.

LYSIMON:

(to himself) I see through this artifice.

HONORÉ:

The wisest sometimes have their moments of caprice. Only he must take a less harsh tone.

LYSIMON:

I don't fathom this obscure persiflage. I've easily unveiled the secret source. Everywhere I recognize the error that dominates you. I see you surrounded by seductive counselors. But friendship remains to you, and vengeful remorse will soon lead virtue into your soul. I will no longer see you the slave of a woman, distracted by love, faithless to honor exposing yourself throughout a century without modesty, and abjuring the nobility of a respectable name, to rise up in a cowardly manner at the feet of a Mistress.

HONORÉ:

You might offend me with all these vain outbursts, with all this false heat, which doesn't impose on me. I will say only one word to you. Rosalie is at home. She could, with a single glance, confound your zeal which takes you too far from your own dwelling.

LYSIMON:

I am staying here, and you know what's right. But do you believe that the passion to do you a service would ever impose on me a greater sacrifice? Too well, I see the ascendant hereabouts. What an air of contagion one breathes hereabouts. But I see your perils, I am necessary to you. Sincere friendship won't be rebuffed. In this time of error you may misunderstand me, this pressing interest which dominates my heart. You won't see me sensitive to this outrage. I want to measure my courage against your danger. And were your imprudent wrath to fall on me, I must ravish you from dishonor despite yourself.

SOPHANES:

(to Honoré) Truly, this is carrying delirium to extreme.

HONORÉ:

(to Rosalie, who enters) Come, come here. Defend yourself. He's too hard to manage. If possible, make his confusion equal his obstinacy. Reveal yourself; let him blush in seeing you, so beautiful. I swear to you, before his eyes, an eternal ardor.

ROSALIE:

(to Lysimon) Eh! What! You please yourself to surprise me in this way. I didn't expect to find you here. But don't pretend not to know me. Perhaps your resentment will calm. What subject do you complain against me? May I not freely dispose of my faith?

LYSIMON:

They warned me of the dazzle of your charms. Seeing you, I experience new worries. I don't pride myself on insensibility. And I know the homage one owes to beauty. I am not defending myself against it. This lovable face will render its weakness excusable in other eyes. As for myself, I could pardon a mistake; but he has plans reproved by honor. See to what dangers his passion exposes him. One day, perhaps, his heart will hate the cause. Foresee these misfortunes, and you yourself, today, lend him a generous support against you. Agree to advice for the good of you both. From prudence, renounce the gift he wishes to make to you. Or fear that soon a sad clarity may unveil to his eyes the frightful truth.

ROSALIE:

I won't listen any further. I have little fear of the threat. Still, I agree that this tone is embarrassing to me. And, at least, you could better hide your humor. Does Honoré have a master? Are you his tutor? What are your rights over him?

LYSIMON:

Those of a faithful friend. And that was enough to excite my zeal. But to recall to him what he owes to his rank, I have still other rights and interests of blood.

HONORÉ:

Lysimon, that's too much.

LYSIMON:

No, I dare to predict that reason will regain its empire over you.

ROSALIE:

(to Lysimon) Are you coming to the ball?

LYSIMON:

(coldly) Yes, if need be.

ROSALIE:

The furor to oblige cannot go any further. This will be amusing.

SOPHANES:

Very amusing.

(Enter Clorinde, Erminie, Marton, dressed to serve.)

CLORINDE:

(to Rosalie) Ah, my dear, don't scold us. You seem to be in a pet. We haven't lost the minutest minute. You can judge by our attire. They say the ball will be so magnificent, memorable forever— Good evening, Mr. Honoré.

SOPHANES:

(to Honoré on one side of the stage) Lysimon promised you revelations. He himself may have fabricated these fictions. Friendship never has such threatening passion.

HONORÉ:

(to Rosalie, in an uneasy tone) In my eyes, Rosalie is only more touching.

ERMINIE:

But we didn't see the carriage below.

ROSALIE:

Oh, Mondor is punctual and won't be late.

CLORINDE:

I hope so. By the way, they say he's preparing a rare marvel for next Friday.

ROSALIE:

What's that?

CLORINDE:

An opera they say, of the utmost beauty, an astonishing spectacle, with choruses in the latest fashion even, whose libretto is very much praised.

ROSALIE:

(calling a lackey) Marin! Rush this evening to secure me a box at the opera. Try to get the first row. Don't forget to go there. Nothing amuses me as much as seeing a new work in full bloom. (to Honoré) Will you accompany me?

HONORÉ:

Do you doubt it?

ERMINIE:

(to Rosalie) My beauty— (low, pointing to Lysimon) We will leave too late. Who's that werewolf?

ROSALIE:

(low to Erminie) A relative of Honoré. A sort of madman.

CLORINDE:

(to Rosalie) Mondor has surely forgotten his word.

ROSALIE:

It's his treacherous gambling; his cursed lottery.

LYSIMON:

(aside, with a feeling of sorrow) Eh! If Honoré doesn't open his eyes in the end?

HONORÉ:

(fondly, to Rosalie) For you this ball is very dear, very precious? Well! Why's Mondor necessary to you? Truly, I don't have my usual coach, but since this morning, obliged to run about, I am using a substitute and I can offer it to you.

ERMINIE:

Truly, we will accept it with gratitude.

CLORINDE:

He's always nice and full of complaisance.

ROSALIE:

Let the coachman get ready as fast as possible, Marton.

(Marton leaves. A Lackey enters.)

LACKEY:

This letter is addressed to Mr. Lysimon.

(The Lackey leaves after delivering the letter to Lysimon.)

LYSIMON:

(joyfully, after having perused the letter) Ah! Finally, I can breathe. Dear Honoré, up to this point I hoped that, wounded by this tone of indecency, you would reproach yourself for the shame of your passion. This last dart, at least is going to clear your eyes. Read, undeceive yourself of an unworthy trick. They boasted to you of the brilliant sacrifice of Milord Calenfort. This letter is from him.

SOPHANES:

(covering his embarrassment with a tone of persiflage) No question it arrives from London today?

ROSALIE:

(in the same tone but a bit uncertain) Your supposition by chance is publicly known. Calenfort has departed.

LYSIMON:

You must have thought that; myself, this morning, I thought so, too. But how to challenge the witness that's here? (to Honoré) Read this.

HONORÉ:

(uneasily, and scornfully, he remains unsure) You wish it—you must be satisfied. But beware—

LYSIMON:

(with nobility) Respect the friend who enlightens you.

CLORINDE:

Where can all this squabble be leading?

ERMINIE:

Right! You will see all this will be cleared up at the Ball. (to Marton, who is returning) Well, Marton?

MARTON:

This man is truly very strange. He has a rare tenderness for his horses. He says they cannot take you.

COACHMAN:

(entering) No, my word. Lose control of yourself, sir, beat me, kill me. I love my horses too much, each has his fancy.

ROSALIE:

Will you look at such insolence.

COACHMAN:

(suddenly struck by Rosalie and observing her with the greatest surprise) Eh! That's my sister, Javotte.

ROSALIE:

(with feigned indignation, mixed with a great deal of trouble) Who are you—my brother? You!

COACHMAN:

What! You are no longer my sister. If my lowliness troubles you to the depths of your heart, mine is really disturbed even more by your magnificence.

HONORÉ:

(confounded) O Heaven! Where was my blind imprudence leading me!

ROSALIE:

(with the most vivid emotion, leaning on Sophanes) I am humiliated enough! Take me away from here. I intend to hide myself forever from my own eyes.

COACHMAN:

(placing himself in front of Rosalie who moves away) I see that you are scorning your brother from pride. It's for me to blush; respect my misery. At least it is honest.

ERMINIE:

(as she leads Clorinde away) I pity her. Still, let's agree that the Ball would have been less amusing.

HONORÉ:

(hurling himself in Lysimon's arms) Ah, my dear Lysimon. What was my delirium?

LYSIMON:

Heaven gave you a heart easy to seduce. Come, let friendship console you over this day—and save you forever from the errors of love!

CURTAIN

ABOUT THE TRANSLATOR

Frank J. Morlock has written and translated many plays since retiring from the legal profession in 1992. His translations have also appeared on Project Gutenberg, the Alexandre Dumas Père web page, Literature in the Age of Napoléon, Infinite Artistries.com, and Munsey's (formerly Blackmask). In 2006 he received an award from the North American Jules Verne Society for his translations of Verne's plays. He lives and works in México.

www.ingramcontent.com/pod-product-compliance
Lightning Source LLC
LaVergne TN
LVHW041622070426
835507LV00008B/398